Lessons From the Sticker Patch

Pastor Cindy,

Thank you for your faithful service to our Lord.

Sheri England

Matt. 16:15

Lessons from the Sticker Patch is a book that will stick to your soul. Shari England weaves biblical truth throughout her colorful narrative, and the result is a book that will help the reader catch a fresh glimpse of God and His immeasurable love in unique ways.

—Wade Burleson, Pastor, Emmanuel Baptist Church, Enid, Oklahoma

Lessons from the Sticker Patch describes the unique childhood experiences of many of us who grew up in northwest Oklahoma. However, Shari has gone beyond nostalgia by sharing the spiritual insights that she has learned along the way.

You will find yourself drawn to this book often. In your private moments, you will find it to be an inspiring book for personal devotions as well as a rich resource of wonderful material for those times when you are called upon to lead a public devotion. I expect I will often be going to Lessons from the Sticker Patch each time my grandchildren ask, "Grandma, what was it like when you were a kid?"

—Mona Loewen, Waukomis, Oklahoma

SHARI ENGLAND

Lessons From the Sticker Patch

RECOGNIZING **GOD'S IMMEASURABLE LOVE** IN EVERYDAY LIFE

TATE PUBLISHING *& Enterprises*

Published by Tate Publishing & Enterprises, LLC
127 E. Trade Center Terrace | Mustang, Oklahoma 73064 USA
1.888.361.9473 | www.tatepublishing.com

Tate Publishing is committed to excellence in the publishing industry. The company reflects the philosophy established by the founders, based on Psalm 68:11,
"The Lord gave the word and great was the company of those who published it."

Book design copyright © 2010 by Tate Publishing, LLC. All rights reserved.
Cover design by Kandi Evans
Interior design by Stefanie Rooney

Published in the United States of America

ISBN: 978-1-61566-727-7
1. Religion, Christian Life, Inspirational
2. Religion, Christian Life, Devotional
10.01.19

Dedication

This book is dedicated to the many loved ones with whom God has so graciously surrounded me.

It is also dedicated to the precious family of my organ donor. The tragic death of their loved one gave me the opportunity for a second chance at life though the gift of organ transplantation. Though we have never met, I think of you so very often.

And to my Lord and Savior, the one whose death provides abundant life on earth and eternal life with Him.

Acknowledgments

There are so many I wish to acknowledge, not only in the creation of this book, but also in the development and refinement of my faith. God has been so gracious in the arrangement of the pieces of my life, dispensing mercy, grace, comfort, and peace, even correction through family and friends as well as my brothers and sisters in Christ.

To Chuck, my husband of thirty-one years: our marriage is truly a testimony of God's amazing grace. I so valued your patience during the lengthy creation of this book, but even more, your unending devotion throughout the anxious moments of our life. I love you dearly.

To my incredible children: Cory, Cole, and Kaci. You are my joy, my delight, and just straight-up fun! You had to grow up more quickly than many your age during my long illness, but I believe God has blessed the strength, courage, and quiet endurance you each demonstrated.

To Mom and Dad: your encouragement, loving support, and faithfulness throughout every stage of my life have meant so very much to me. Additionally, life on the farm offered excellent life lessons, as well as great fodder for storytelling! "The lines have fallen to me in pleasant places; indeed, my heritage is beautiful to me" (Psalm 16:6).

To my beautiful sister, Debbie: Your passionate

belief in my personal endeavors has always encouraged me, and your clear-cut candor is delightfully refreshing. What a blessing to have you as both sister and best friend.

To Delane and Sandy Reimer: you are so very dear to our family. With Christ as your example, you truly have been faithful imitators of God. May He bless you always.

To Rick and Jarita Cardwell: thank you for your faith, support, and assistance in making sure my vision of a book became a reality. God bless you as you have blessed us.

To Mona Lowen: I so appreciate your assistance in the completion of the manuscript. You quieted the storm of many of my writing apprehensions.

To Korina, publisher and editor of the *North Central Reporter:* thank you for the opportunity to publish my column each week, essentially becoming the springboard for this book. God bless you as you continue to honor Him in all you do.

To the wonderful people of Grant and Kay counties in northern Oklahoma: your prayers and support were instrumental in my healing during the difficult years of my illness and multiple hospitalizations. I am forever mindful of all you did for my family and me in our darkest days.

I also feel a sense of gratitude for our local Christian radio, KLVV, 88.7 FM out of Ponca City, Oklahoma. In 1992, choosing to put myself on a Christian music diet, I searched the radio for a Christian station. Unaware that KLVV had been on for only a few months, immediately I came upon their channel. From their programming, my faith grew and my understanding deepened through music that glorified God and teaching that edified its listeners. May God continue to bless the faithful ministry of KLVV.

"Surely goodness and mercy have followed me all the days of my life" (Psalm 23:6).

Table of Contents

"And these things I write unto you, that our joy may be made complete."

First John 1:4

Introduction

Growing up on the farm, Oklahoma grass stickers were a common assailant for the barefoot pedestrian. Like a baby calf without his mama, the cry of one caught in the confines of the sticker patch was a familiar one. Young or old, all victims assumed the same helpless stance as they carefully turned their bodies, searching for rescue.

Unaware of the covert calamity that lay hidden in the grass, most incidents caught victims completely off guard. Escape resembled strategic soldiers in a field of active landmines, with every step deliberate and calibrated.

"Consider it all joy, my brethren, when you encounter various trials" (James 1:2). Consider it joy? Trials can be painful, difficult, abrupt, and unexpected—just like stickers. Many times we ask, "Why me? How could this have happened?"

From the trials of life to the temptations of the flesh, the sticker patch is an amusing parallel to our reaction and response to those "stickery" moments. The difference is that the pain of testing will produce a stronger, more purposeful faith, while the pain associated with temptation is always a result of sin, bringing forth festering wounds and the casualties of sin.

We often are led to believe that the life of the Christian is utter bliss, like a smooth, free-flowing melody, one hymn after another. But there are days that feel far from liberated and anything but melodious, days when you wonder if other believers are going through the same battles you are. Moments you question your faith and even question God.

For this reason, I hope the reader will relate to these personal stories drawn from the infusion of my life journey with my faith journey. Throughout my life, I have sensed the hand of God guiding and protecting me, whether during the willful trek down the smooth path of rebellion or the often-rough terrain of the obedient faith walk. He is truly the ever-loving and ever-present Guide and Comforter.

My journey with God began at the tender age of eight, sensing that God had called me for "something great." In a moment of youthful spiritual reflection, I heard the words similar to what I later found in Scripture. Jeremiah 33:3 says, "Call to Me and I will answer you, and I will tell you great and mighty things which you do not know."

Lacking full understanding, however, my *call* turned a corner in my teen years. As a child, I dreamed of becoming a ballerina. In my teens, I was encouraged to consider modeling, and I began that pursuit during my first year of college. My career path soon diverted when I instead chose to get married. Even so, almost by accident, my dream of modeling did materialize for a few years when our boys were still quite young. It was fun for a short time, but I became weary of having to measure up to someone else's standards of beauty. It was not all I had dreamed it might be, and it certainly did not fill the emptiness within me.

My constant pursuit for happiness took me to a virtual hell and back. It was in the darkness, however, that I found the Light! Jesus Christ, the true light, followed me into my darkest place and offered me the freedom that comes only through reaching out to the one who is the way, the truth, and the life. This time I understood Jeremiah 33:3.

God's call for each of us is to "call out to Him" so that He might show us things far greater than we are or will ever hope to be in our own strength. His ways are so much higher than our ways, but our lack of divine perception prevents us from understanding that "the Lord's hand is not so short that it cannot save; nor His ear so dull that it cannot hear" (Isaiah 59:1).

I have always loved the way Jesus taught using parables. To some it was a good story, to others, a spiritual truth with a deeper message woven into illustrations using His creation. It is my desire to administer the truth of God's Word through these parable-like messages, simple as they may seem at times, that together we can "consider it all joy" as we come to know the breadth, length, depth, and height of the love of Christ.

Just as the tiny thorns of the sticker patch embed deeply into our tender flesh, so too do the memories of our thorny trials and stinging temptations embed deeply into our tender souls. We may forget the intensity of the initial pain, but we will indeed remember the extent and effects of the experiences. They make us who we are today, while preparing us for the greater purpose of God's perfect plan for our tomorrow—all for the glory of God.

> "Our worship for the glorious Lord is an unchained melody in the ears of our Abba Father, joined in harmony by a body of believers, keeping rhythm with the heartbeat of the living and breathing Spirit of God."

—Shari England

In My Father's Arms

In the early 1960s, northern Oklahoma endured several especially bitter winters. The frosty wet flurries were a natural kid magnet, so for six snowbound and restless children, dry gloves were in steady high demand. With necessity the mother of invention, many times in place of gloves we would layer thick socks over our hands. One frigid afternoon, my brothers, sister, and I were playing in the snow-filled sandbox. They began to get cold and decided to go inside. At the stubborn age of six, I was willing to tough it out.

I was so absorbed in my play and determined to finish my snow castle, I had not noticed my socks/gloves were soaking wet. The outer layer was not only wet but had also become heavy, with little frozen pieces clinging to the ends dangling several inches past my fingertips. Having become quite awkward in the completion of my project, I removed the socks from my hands.

How much better it now seemed to no longer be encumbered by such a hindering piece of clothing. I now had full use of my fingers, giving me the creative freedom I didn't realize was possible while wearing socks on my hands. Within minutes, however, I began to notice I could no longer feel my fingers. I could barely even move them. Bending my fingers was painful, and though I tried, I could not get my "gloves" back on. In my stubbornness, I had waited too long. I felt helpless as I stared at my stiff, throbbing fingers.

Then I saw him—my rescuer, my fixer of everything, my knight in dirty cowboy boots—my dad! I immediately burst into tears.

"Daddy!" I cried. "My hands hurt so bad."

He did not scold me for staying out too long. He did not tell me how foolish I was for taking my gloves off. The look in his eyes was that of compassion and tenderness. He scooped me up into his arms and carried me inside.

The fire was roaring in the old living room stove. Sitting there together before the fire, he repeatedly cupped his hands around mine, held them as close as he could to the warmth, and then gently closed them around my cold and lifeless hands. After a few minutes, I slowly began to feel life return to my frozen fingers. The painful throbbing had stopped, and I tested my fingers, opening and then closing them again … and again.

I wish I could say I learned my lesson that day in the snowy sandbox, but there would be other times when I would again suffer the painful consequences of a stubborn self-will. The rebellious spirit of the flesh and its attempt to fill the void left from the failed promises of a self-seeking and godless world often brings bitter and lifeless results.

I have always felt the greatest strengths of a man are his tenderness and gentleness. The same calloused hands of my father that toiled unceasingly around the farm gingerly buckled my shoes and tied my bows on Sunday mornings. Those seemingly unimportant things did not go without notice.

The most precious thing my dad showed me that day in the sandbox was not just his tenderness and love toward me but also the tender mercy of a loving heavenly Father. I often wonder if there are those who struggle with the love and acceptance of our heavenly Father because they did not feel the acceptance of an earthly father. I am thankful for that demonstration, thus giving me a deeper, richer understanding of the one I call Father, my rescuer, fixer of everything, my Lord and Savior, Jesus Christ.

Abba Father, You are our shepherd; we shall not be in want. You are our shelter, our deliverer, our comforter, and our refuge. With gentleness and tenderness, You lead us back into the fold when we have gone astray. You lift us high above our trials that we may give You the glory and exalt Your name forever. You are mighty God, Prince of Peace, the Lamb of God, and Father to the fatherless, and we are Your beloved. Amen.

Ballerina in a Box

She was beauty, elegance, and grace. Balancing faultlessly on one toe, she spun slowly to the dainty twinkling tune of the "ballerina" melody. Occasionally hanging up on one particular note, she quickly regained her position to continue her magnificent endless performance. At least that was until I closed the lid.

A ballerina in a box—she was still the most beautiful thing I had seen, and I dreamed of being just like her. Secretly, I hated shutting her up in the box. I would eventually learn you can never really close the lid on a dream.

I was six years old when I received the pink jewelry box with a tutu-clad ballet dancer as its centerpiece. Soon I was looking for tutu alternatives in fabric, towels, even a blow-up swim ring. I tried numerous attempts of standing on my toes; however, Red Ball tennis shoes did not make the grade when it came to pirouettes. I practiced the walk, the arabesques, and the feet changes I had observed in the dancers on television. I could feel the dream unfolding inside me. In my mind, I was a ballerina!

I'm not sure what it was that attracted me to the fascination of the ballerina. My guess would be what it is all little girls admire—the gracefulness and elegance as well as the talent and agility of standing on one toe while spinning at the same time. The ballerina seemed to exhibit strength, dignity, and composure, always poised for the next graceful move.

In time, however, my pink jewelry box, along with my swim-ring tutu, made its fated journey into the "Land of the Lost." Those dreamy visions of ballerina slippers and tutus took a back seat to basketball shoes and pom-poms throughout the majority of my school years.

During my senior year of high school, my English teacher offered a course in creative writing. I enjoyed it immensely, and surprisingly, won a college scholarship in a true-life story contest sponsored by a popular magazine.

"Keep writing," she urged me the week of high school graduation.

Keep writing? About what?

The years following would lead me through paths of opportunities as well as roadblocks and difficulties, teaching me of true beauty, strength, grace, and humility. All the while, I would occasionally pick up a pen and paper and jot down my thoughts, many times in the form of poetry. Sadly, I did not take it seriously and either lost or tossed much of what I had written.

Throughout my wavering life, whether faithful or fickle, God, who is always faithful, has graciously granted me precious tokens of His divine providence, in spite of my waywardness. Reminding me often of His promises and His call on my life, He has continually shown me particular areas that would hang me up, and I quickly returned to my position in Christ.

"Therefore having been justified by faith, we have peace with God through our Lord Jesus Christ, through whom also we have obtained our introduction by faith into this grace in which we stand; and we exult in hope of the glory of God" (Romans 5:1–2).

Over the years, God slowly but faithfully reopened the lid on my box of dreams, although His plans were so much better than anything I had ever imagined. He went exceeding abundantly beyond anything I ever asked or even imagined. (Eph. 3:20)

"And being fully assured that what He had promised, He was able also to perform" (Romans 4:21).

I never learned to do a graceful arabesque or the perfect pirouette. God did not desire for me to be a beautiful ballerina balancing on one toe and spinning in one place, but rather to be a spirit-filled child of God grounded in truth and walking in love. Such is His desire for each of us.

God of all glory, majesty, honor, and power, Your ways are so much higher than our ways; Your thoughts are so much higher than our thoughts, but You come down to where we are and meet us in our place of need. Help us to daily walk in Your grace as we seek to accomplish Your will for our lives each day, becoming the person of Your perfect design. In Jesus's name, amen.

Petals of Performance

The sunflower, though beautiful in its own right, is a rather large and clumsy flower. It does not give off a pleasant floral scent and is hard to dress up with greenery and baby's breath. With a rather "meaty" center, the sunflower is not usually the flower of choice to press between the pages of a book amid the delicate rose or tender violets.

I love to watch a field of large sunflowers as their dark brown faces the size of paper plates and the yellow petal frames turn with the sun as it moves from low in the morning to high noon to evening sunset. Thousands in the field of faces turn toward the sun, thus the name *sunflower*.

When I was ten years old, the fate of my future mate lay in the innocent petals of the sunflower. My sister and I stripped many a flower, hoping to win the affection of an unsuspecting young beau.

"He loves me, he loves me not. He loves me, he loves me not."

With experience, we learned how to manipulate the petals, picking two instead of one, or sometimes counting the little petals and then not counting them, depending on their significance. If the outcome was bleak, we just tossed the flower and started over. Though we realized there was truly nothing magical about the petals, in theory it was a great idea, just not very realistic.

We can tend to play the same game when it comes to our position in Christ. For a number of years, I felt that God's love for me depended upon my performance or accomplishments. I would do some godly work and feel His delight, then I would mess up and assume His displeasure. By my actions I was playing, "He loves me, He loves me not!"

I even tried manipulation by picking and choosing what I felt was a sin, discounting "little sins" and doubling up on spiritual activity to win the affection of Almighty God. I also attempted "starting over" a couple of times, thinking I would surely get it right the next time. Like the petal-picked sunflower, I felt stripped, as the petals of performance lay scattered around me.

God's love for us is not determined by the amount of work we do for Him. In the Apostle Paul's letter to the Ephesians, he encouraged spiritual maturity in believers, urging them to be more aware of their position in Christ and to draw upon Him daily.

"But God, being rich in mercy, because of His great love ... made us alive together with Christ ... For by grace you have been saved through faith; and that not of yourselves, it is the gift of God; not as a result of works, so that no one may boast" (Ephesians 2:4–5, 8–9).

We can work our way up the ladder of success; we can even work our way up in the church. However, we cannot work our way into salvation. The works we do will be a direct outflow of a personal relationship with Jesus Christ, through whom we have redemption and forgiveness of sins. We grow and build our faith by surrounding ourselves with others who hunger and thirst for righteousness and by attaining godly wisdom and instruction through the word of God as well as through multiple Christian resources available today. From early sunrise to evening sunset, turn your face toward the Son.

Blessed Lord, just as the face of the sunflower moves with the sun, I pray our eyes may be set upon You. Thank you for the amazing grace that allows us to be seated in the heavenly places in Christ Jesus, and for making us alive together with Christ. There is no limit to Your love, Father. It is from everlasting to everlasting. In Jesus's name, amen.

Life through Double Doors

What is it about double doors? They possess no magical powers; most are made of solid wood, others maybe of aluminum or even glass. I have noticed, however, that a few doors throughout my life seemed to represent a rite of passage as I moved from one stage of life into another. It is as if life's most significant moments must first pass through double doors.

The first set of double doors in my memory was of a light-colored wood with long, slender windows near the centers. These doors were part of my introduction to my faith. They were the doors to my first church as a young child.

Even the elementary school bus had double doors. We rode one of these every morning for what seemed a hundred years. What always fascinated me about these doors was that one door swung one way and the other swung the opposite way. What can I say? I was easily entertained!

The next set of double doors was the entrance into my days of junior high and high school. They were of a very heavy metal, which took some effort to open, closely representative of the struggles that tend to accompany the teen years.

A few years later I found myself arm in arm with my dad, standing behind double doors made of dark wood that swung open toward the church sanctuary decorated with flowers, bows, and candles. We were awaiting the sound of the bridal march. I noticed he had tears in his eyes.

Only a couple years later, I would find myself moving very quickly through another set of double doors. These were very large, very cold, aluminum double doors as nurses rushed me into the delivery room for the birth of our firstborn. We enjoyed this so much we did it two more times.

There would be more encounters with double doors throughout the years. Some we walked boldly through; others we felt as though we crawled. With each experience, however, came a clearer understanding, sharper awareness, deeper wisdom and knowledge, unspeakable joy, and sometimes a great deal of heartache—the true test of unconditional love.

Maybe it is a silly observation, but for whatever reason, these doors have become deeply rooted into my memory. Perhaps they are simply a reminder of where I have been and where I am going. To borrow the expression of a pastor I heard years ago, "I'm not where I need to be, but praise God I'm not where I used to be." Hindsight also allows us to look back and say, "Surely the Lord was in this place, and we did not know it." (Gen. 28:16)

God is faithful at every stage of our life and apportions to us what He desires, as we are able to handle it. First Thessalonians 5:24 says, "Faithful is He who calls you, and He also will bring it to pass."

Father God, thank you that You are faithful to complete in us that which You have started. Thank you that even when we act in disobedience, as Your children, You still watch over us, even arranging the doors of our lives in such a manner as to bring us back to You. Forgive us for the times we have failed to be faithful, Father. We recognize that our faithfulness is the fruit of Your Spirit at work in our lives. May others see Your faithfulness revealed in us. In Jesus's name, amen.

Letting Go

In elementary school, lunch recess was a time of organized chaos. Following lunch, a throng of chattering, squealing voices eagerly converged upon an overly trampled playground as teachers dutifully stood their post as medic, jury, and executioners of justice.

Recess is a child's introduction to survival of the fittest. As a child, I was small and fast, which worked well in some competitions, but featherweights usually are chosen last in the game of Red Rover, the chain game where players try to break through the opponent's chain, tightly linked together by the clasping of hands. Red Rover sent chills up my spine knowing they considered me one of the weak links.

The object of the game was to "capture" the strong ones from the other side. If you were small, you knew the opponent would naturally try to break through *your* part of the chain, the weakest link! And there was one player that would absolutely paralyze me as I would watch him scoping out the possibilities, eyeing my link in particular.

Playground discernment comes through past injuries. We learned that holding too tightly was actually detrimental, as the massive opponent plowed through, sometimes bringing down one whole section of the chain. When a rather large contender from the other side neared, our previous injuries educated us simply to unclasp before contact, at times causing the mammoth to plunge head first into the dirt. We may have lost that round but we saved an arm or two. When you are small, you have to think for yourself.

Throughout our lives, we will meet with a myriad of confrontations—illness, abandonment, injustice, etc. The bonds we make with our friends and loved ones create a strong chain of security and support when life bombards us with impending assailants. It is a chain of loyalty, dependability and faithfulness; one in which we will often rely.

Occasionally however, our tendency will be to tense up, brace ourselves, and grip as tightly as possible for fear of losing something deemed precious or valuable. Real or imagined, the threat of loss can be devastating, and we become paralyzed as the challenger stares us down. Sometimes, holding too tightly could prove to do more harm than good, not only to ourselves, but also to those to which we hold. Maturity, experience, and godly wisdom teach us when to hold on and when to let go.

Scripture tells of the exhausting lineup of conspiracy, mistreatment, and injustice in the life of

Joseph after his own brothers stripped him of his special tunic, threw him in a pit, and sold him into slavery. Though Joseph may not have fully understood everything in those dark moments, he did understand his place with God. It is hard to imagine one's own family turning on you as Joseph's did; but remaining faithful to God's call, Joseph allowed God to work mightily through his circumstances.

Genesis 50:20 records the words of Joseph to his brothers: "And as for you, you meant evil against me, but God meant it for good in order to bring about this present result."

On the schoolyard of life, choose carefully the connections you create. Be aware of the importance that each link works to strengthen and encourage you in your faith. Often, the strength of our chain will actually work to halt a coming assailant, even thwarting its malicious tactics. Additionally, communicate well with others so that those linked to you can best coordinate and pray with you in your struggle.

There will come those times, however, when we simply need to let go and allow the will of God to manifest in our lives. Romans 8:28 says, "And we know that God causes all things to work together for good to those who love God, to those who are called according to His purpose."

"But we also exult in our tribulations, knowing that tribulation brings about perseverance; and perseverance, proven character; and proven character, hope; and hope does not disappoint, because the love of God has been poured out within our hearts through the Holy Spirit who was given to us" (Romans 5:3–5).

Finally beloved, rejoice, because you will be stronger than you were before. What was intended for our harm, God can and will use for your good and His glory!

Thank you, God, for giving us the victory through our Lord and Savior Jesus Christ! Jesus's death on the cross and His resurrection from the grave assure us of victory in this life and in the life to come. Forgive us, Father, for the times we have allowed fear, doubt, and circumstances to defeat us. Help us to recognize the higher calling in every situation, that we might be used for a greater purpose. It is faith that gives us the victory to overcome the world and overcome our giants. To God be all the glory!

Trust and Obey

Though my mother held no college degree, she was an amazing teacher. At a very young age, her ability at the sewing machine completely captivated me. So little by little, she began instructing me in the craft of sewing. As genetics would have it, Mom and I were both sticklers for detail, so we were a good match as teacher and student.

I learned to pay attention to every notch and marking and to follow the pattern guide precisely. Most important was the preparation and layout of the patterns in order to have the best possible foundation for my creation. In addition to that, pin, pin, pin, and pin some more in order to hold my project together until permanently stitched.

The greatest thing she did as teacher was demonstrate her confidence and belief in me. She would make sure I had everything going in the right direction, and before walking away, she would always add, "I know you can do this!" She did not stay and hover

over me but instead went back to the work in which she previously had been engaged.

I remember at times being somewhat fearful at her leaving, but I also remember feeling empowered. I truly believed that if she trusted me enough to leave the room, she must also truly believe I could handle the challenge. My mother did well in teaching me the powerful principles of trust and obedience. She trusted me with all her sewing tools and machines, as well as my ability to follow the guides as she taught. Likewise, I fully trusted her knowledge and understanding of what she taught, and I closely followed all her instructions, knowing that I could still call on her at any moment.

Scripture also teaches us of the powerful principles of trust and obedience, along with the peace that accompanies the faithful and obedient heart. Additionally, it teaches that God will not allow anything to come into our lives that we are not capable of withstanding.

"No temptation has overtaken you except such as is common to man; but God is faithful, who will not allow you to be tempted beyond what you are able, but with the temptation will also provide a way of escape also, that you may be able to endure it" (1 Corinthians 10:13).

Just as one can be tempted to sin, one can also be tempted to doubt God's sovereignty.

When I became gravely ill, there were times when at first I questioned whether I was able to handle such an enormous challenge. I also remember specifically the day God reminded me of what my mother had taught me as a young seamstress, and something clicked in my head.

Immediately I became empowered and, oddly enough, rather excited when I stopped to realize that God must trust me completely to allow me to bear such a difficult burden. Thankfully, I had spent several years in "faith training" in the word of God, so I had an excellent foundation in place and was fully prepared with all the directions and instructions I could possibly need. In addition, I learned to pray, pray, pray, and pray some more, as prayer was a necessity in holding it all together in those days. I simply trusted and obeyed.

Often our doubt is a sign of our own spiritual immaturity and lack of faith. Conquering doubt demands a growing, obedient relationship with God. "So faith comes from hearing, and hearing by the word of Christ" (Romans 10:17).

Trusting the wisdom of my mother enabled me to easily accept every level of her training, eventually strengthening my level of confidence, along with increased skill. Likewise, our trust in God strengthens and increases our level of faith and ability. "Trust in the Lord with all your heart and do not lean on your own understanding. In all your ways acknowledge Him, and He will make your paths straight" (Prov. 3:5).

Doubt is destructive. God knows this and wants us to know it too. "The Lord gives grace and glory; no good thing does He withhold from those who walk uprightly. O Lord of hosts, how blessed is the man who trusts in Thee!" (Psalm 84:11–12)

Holy God, like a shepherd, You lead me to green pastures and quiet waters and restore my soul. You walked with me through my valley of the shadow of death and comforted me in my sorrow. You prepared me with Your promises in the presence of bad news and anointed me with Your healing oil. My cup surely overflows from Your goodness and kindness, and I will tell of Your wonders all the days of my life. Amen.

Junkyard Peachtree

A popular phrase among believers tells us to "grow where we are planted." The key principle in this is that rather than complaining about where we are, we should do our best in the present condition. True... to a point.

Waste management on the farm years ago was typically a burn pit in the pasture. Everything including the kitchen sink ended up in the burn pit. While on one of our usual outings through the adventurous terrain of the pasture, my siblings and I observed a tree with bright orange spots in the distance. Upon closer look, we discovered that a rogue peach tree bearing the fullest, plumpest, largest peaches we had ever seen had sprung up in the middle of a pile of scrap iron and other refuse along the edge of the burn pit.

That summer, we reveled in fresh peach slices, peach cobbler, peach jam, and preserves. If it could be made with peaches, Mom prepared it. With the peach tree finally stripped bare, we looked forward to the next year's harvest of more junkyard peaches. To our disappointment, however, it would be the first and last harvest that tree would produce. Like the one-hit wonder song of the 70s "Precious and Few," our one and only peach tree would never bloom again.

The story reminds me of the "Parable of the Sower" from the Gospel of Mark (Mark 4:3–20). Jesus spoke about the terrestrial placement of the seed as the sower cast it. Some seed fell beside the road, some on rocky ground, and other seed fell among the thorns. Still other seed fell into good soil. He continued with, "He who has ears to hear, let him hear" (Mark 4:9).

He then explained the parable to His followers and the twelve disciples.

> The sower sows the word. The seed beside the road are the ones who when the word is sown and they hear, immediately Satan comes and steals it. Similarly, the seed sown on rocky places are those who, when they hear the word, immediately receive it with joy; but because it is not firmly planted, are only temporary and they immediately fall away. The seed sown among the thorns are those who hear the word, but the worries of the world and the desire for other things choke the word and it becomes unfruitful. And the seed

sown into good soil are those who hear the word and accept it and bear fruit, thirty, sixty and a hundredfold.

Mark 4:14–20

Our "flash from the trash" peach tree surely never had a chance, considering its surroundings of scrap iron, broken toys, and worn tires. It obviously found the footing it needed for one good hoorah but lacked the surroundings of fertility to bear fruit continuously.

The question for us as believers is, "What kind of soil is the Word falling upon in your life?" If you struggle with receiving the Word, find a mature believer who can pray with you and who will bathe you in prayer as the eyes of your understanding begin to open.

Maybe you are one who was all excited when you first decided to follow Christ but never really followed up with church attendance or Bible study, and you quickly lost interest. Perhaps life dealt you some harsh blows. You consumed yourself with worry, anger, or disappointment, and now you are not even sure of your faith anymore. Jesus watches for you to return and eagerly awaits you with open arms.

Life does not always place us exactly where we thought we would be. Oftentimes we end up in a place that seems counter to our natural surroundings. Like the peach seed, we may be able to flourish temporarily but will eventually flounder amid unhealthy surroundings. Godly wisdom will work to seek out an environment that provides depth and stability for long-lasting fruitfulness.

While it is true that we should grow where we are planted, we need to make sure, that our environment is fertile ground, where faith enthusiastically germinates. It has been said, "Do not mistake *activity* for *productivity*," so take care to surround yourself with other believers who are productive in their faith, to encourage you in your walk so that you will produce thirty, sixty, and a hundredfold, bearing good fruit in all you do.

Father, we thank you for Your Word and for the Word, Jesus Christ. We rebuke the lies of Satan and his attempts to steal what we have received. Help us to find good soil, not only to cultivate our faith more effectively, but also that we might sow even more seed from the fruit produced in us. In Jesus's name, amen.

What's in a name?

When I was a young preteen, I had the sudden notion that I wanted to change my name to Marsha. I had a cousin named Marsha, and then, of course, there was the love-struck, starry-eyed older sister from *The Brady Bunch* sitcom of the 70s. That juvenile idea lasted about as long as my wish of ever having Marsha Brady's long, straight hair.

Names tend to run in cycles, with some generations occasionally recognized by specific names. However, names from early twentieth century are now recycling through our newest generation. Biblical names are always in fashion and used to hold particular meaning, typically indicative of either existing personal character or even a prophetic significance.

In the Bible, God occasionally changed the names of individuals for a specific reason. Sometimes the name change came before a divine manifestation or revelation, other times afterward. Abram's name was changed to Abraham *before* he became the "father of many nations." Jacob received his new name *after* he wrestled with God. Jacob's name was changed to Israel, meaning, "having power with God."

Jesus changed Simon's name to Peter *before* he became the "rock." He gave him a name distinct of the moral and spiritual strength into which Simon would eventually develop. Jesus gave him the new name that it might be an incentive to become what Jesus had called him to be.

"I also say to you that you are Peter, and upon this rock I will build My church; and the gates of Hades will not overpower it. I will give you the keys of the kingdom of heaven; whatever you bind on earth will be bound in heaven, and whatever you loose on earth will be loosed in heaven" (Matthew 16:18–19).

When we come into the family of God, we are known by the name of Christian, which literally means "Christ follower." Most of us receive that name before our lives even begin to line up with what God foresees for us. Too often, we certainly do not behave in a Christlike manner.

So are we taking the name of Christ for granted? Do we wear His name like a badge we can remove when we want to appear less spiritual? Can we be called a Christian if we love our sin more than we love our Savior, and heed not His holy Word?

It is impossible for us to grow to become like someone we do not even know. We only grow more like Christ when we deepen our knowledge of Him. The deeper our knowledge, the deeper our understanding will become as well. The more we understand, the more we grow to love Him deeper still.

It is not about wearing the name like a cloak of admirable spirituality. This surely does not honor a holy God. God commands our obedience. He requires sincere devotion. God deserves pure worship and adoration!

Jesus died not that we might be *named* after Him but that we might *live* after Him. He died that we might live with a new name, a new hope, and a divine plan. It is the name that, like Simon, is an incentive to become what Jesus calls us to be. His name is a reminder of our divine inheritance, that we too possess the keys of the kingdom.

Father, we thank you for the saving grace delivered to us through Jesus Christ. Thank you for the opportunity to wear the name of Christ upon our hearts. As a Christ follower, may we be fervent in bringing honor to You in all we do. May Your kingdom come and Your will be done in our hearts, Lord, and may our actions be consistent with Your name. Thank you that Your Word assures us that Your divine plan will be fulfilled in us, even though we do not see it. In Jesus's holy name, amen.

Message in a Jar

I love peanut butter. I have loved it since my child-hood. My dad was and continues to be a peanut butter fanatic. He puts peanut butter on nearly everything, or so it seems, and thick enough to leave teeth marks in the dense spread. I like mine spread v-e-r-y thin.

Years ago, a friendly rivalry ensued between us when a new jar of peanut butter appeared in the cabinet. The challenge was to make the *first dent* in the smooth, untouched layer of the peanut spread. It started with just a finger indention that marked our territory. Then someone got clever.

I remember opening a new jar with the inten-tion of making the first mark. I twisted the lid open, expecting to find that shiny, level surface but instead found the toothpick inscribed message, "Ha ha, I beat you!" with a smiley face underneath. I knew the teasing inscription could only be from my dad, just to let me know he had gotten to the jar before I had.

From that day on, until the day I moved out, we

both enjoyed writing tender, silly, and often teasing messages with a toothpick in the fresh layer of the new jar. It was a bummer for both of us if we found that someone else not as "clever" as we were had the audacity to plunge their knife into *our* peanut butter.

I am sure what made it so special to me was the fact that these were messages from my dad, special messages intended just for me, and I knew each one had an even deeper underlying message. Whether teasing or tender, our jar of peanut butter became a playful method of conveying messages in which we both understood and enjoyed.

Nearly two decades ago, when I began my true spiritual journey, inscribed on the pages of my Bible I found messages for me, intended just for me that day, at that particular time and place in my life. More importantly, these messages came, not from the great prophets or writers of the Bible, but my Daddy God, or Abba Father, as Jesus lovingly called Him.

I have attempted to make it a daily practice to spend time in the Word, but I confess there have been days I have missed for various reasons. But with every moment spent in God's Word, I look forward to discovering something new. Many times I can be reading a scripture I've read before, possibly even underlined or highlighted, but for some reason, on that day a special message will jump off the page. That is the excitement of God's Word. It can be fresh and new every time you open it.

Lamentations 3:22–23 says, "The Lord's loving kindnesses indeed never cease, for His compassions never fail. They are new every morning; great is Thy faithfulness."

Therefore, "let us draw near with a sincere heart in full assurance of our faith … and let us hold fast the confession of our hope without wavering, for He who promised is faithful" (Heb. 10:22–23).

Abba Father, I thank you that Your Word is personal and unique no matter who sits down to read it. You speak to us individually through Your Word. I ask, as Paul did, that each of us would be filled with the knowledge of Your will in all spiritual wisdom and understanding, so we might walk in a manner worthy of the Lord and that we would be continuously increasing in the knowledge of God. Great is Your faithfulness, Father; Your compassions are fresh and new every morning. May the word of God continue to spread as the family of God increases. Amen.

This Little Light of Mine

As children of the midsixties, Vacation Bible School was as much a summertime staple as it is today. To be honest, though, I cannot recall any particular lesson or activity, but I do remember a mountain of dry cookies, weak Kool-Aid, and the customary VBS songs.

We learned "I'm in the Lord's Army," "The B-I-B-L-E," "Jacob's Ladder," "I've Got the Joy," and my favorite, "This Little Light of Mine." I stood amid the young herd as we all sang with our pointer finger waving in the air, "This little light of mine, I'm gonna let it shine."

The song encouraged us to let our light shine among those around us. It also cautioned us of "hiding it under a bushel" and to be aware of Satan's attempts to "blow it out." Though as children we really didn't fully understand "the bushel" or even how Satan might "blow it out," we did have a general idea of letting "this light" shine, and so we sang with boldness. Years later, I still think of the childhood song as I read from the book of Matthew.

"Ye are the light of the world. A city set on a hill cannot be hid. Neither do men light a candle and put it under a bushel, but on the candlestick; and it giveth light to all that are in the house" (Matthew 5:14–25, KJV).

Contemporary versions of the Bible use basket, bucket, peck measure, or even clay pot in place of bushel, but all suggest a covering for the light. A modern-day bushel might even be a metaphor for the attitude of political correctness or the often-mis-construed "separation of church and state".

Then Jesus goes on to say, "Let your light shine before men in such a way that they may see your good works, and glorify your Father who is in heaven" (Matthew 5:16).

Jesus desires for our light to shine through good works in order to lead others to Him, thus glorify-ing the Father. Many times, as Christians, it appears as if we are working undercover. The only appar-ent evidence may be our vehicle parked in front of a church on Sunday morning. I love the clever quip, "If you were arrested today for being a Christian, would there be enough evidence to convict you?"

Jesus is the light we are to share. We cannot shine that light without a personal relationship with Him. He is the Light of the World, the only true source of our light. The light of Christ also reveals our need for a Savior. Christ sees who we are in Him and who we will become. Only Satan reminds us of our past. Jesus Christ is Lord over our past, present, and future! There is liberation in embracing that truth.

Finally, the childhood song stresses light maintenance. Do not be swayed by the comments of unbelievers or even critical religiosity attempting to blow out your candle. It is important to get involved in church and a personal or small-group Bible study, as well as a circle of believers to encourage and support you. Let your light shine brightly wherever your path leads you.

Lord God, Your Word is a lamp unto my feet and a light unto my path. The light of your Word reveals my desperate need and Your perfect salvation. You are the true light for all men. Increase our faith and our confidence, Father, that we may not appear as undercover Christians, but let our light shine freely to all we encounter. Thank you for allowing us to share the light of Christ with others. In Jesus's name, amen.

Oh, Be Careful, Little Mouth

Have you ever noticed that if *we* mess up, it is a temporary lapse of judgment, but if someone else messes up, he or she will be immediately declared a hypocrite and unfit for the kingdom? I once heard a comment by a pastor saying, "We cannot measure Christianity by the conduct of Christians but rather by the conduct of Christ!"

One of my most notorious childhood stories of self-righteousness came out of the daily routine that took place in the opening exercises of grade school during my fourth grade year in 1969. Every morning we stood at attention to recite the flag salute and the Lord's Prayer. Our teacher encouraged us before the prayer to bow our heads and close our eyes.

There was a certain boy in the class most of us considered a source of irritation. He bounced off the walls, rarely brushed his teeth, and had a persistent runny nose. Girls avoided him like the plague, and boys taunted him mercilessly. *Johnny* wanted so desperately just to fit in.

During the morning exercises, I noticed a grave infraction of the "heads bowed, eyes closed" rule. Out of the corner of my eye, I was secretly watching Johnny look around the room during the Lord's Prayer. As soon as we came to "Amen" and began taking our seats, my hand shot up. I felt it was my duty to inform the teacher that there was an irreverent defector among us.

"Mrs. Schuneman, Mrs. Schuneman," I blurted as my hand waved wildly. "Johnny had his eyes open during the prayer!"

I just knew Johnny would be staying inside for recess. I felt I had singlehandedly saved the entire class from the would-be tormenter for the day. I arrogantly sensed the approval of all my classmates as they innocently looked on. Mrs. Schuneman, however, without missing a beat, very calmly returned, "Shari, how did you know?"

Okay, I was young, but I was no dummy. I heard the bars of guilt slam shut in my conscience. I had just hung myself with the rope intended for Johnny. Her question did not demand a verbal response. With gentle wisdom, she tenderly admonished me, but sweltering conviction was throbbing in my head.

Throughout the years, there have been several times when I pulled out the self-righteous rope of condemnation. As Christians, many times we can come across as harsh as a blowtorch instead of the gentle candle God calls us to be. I envision an angel of the Lord coming along after me with a broom and dustpan, sweeping up my messes.

First Corinthians 4:21 says, "Shall I come to you with a rod, or with love and a spirit of gentleness?" Paul reminds us in the third chapter of Second Thessalonians that we are to be gentle even with those who lead undisciplined lives, not considering them an enemy, but rather gently admonishing them as a brother or sister in Christ. The hard part is then leaving the rest of the work to the Holy Spirit to change the heart of the person. The Christian life is indeed a daily work in progress. We will only have arrived when we see Him face-to-face.

Merciful Father, You sent Your Son into the world not to condemn the world but that the world might be saved through Him. Thank you that the Spirit of Christ sets us free from the law of sin and death. Forgive us for the times we really mess up. Help us to be as patient with others, Lord, as You have been with us. Holy Spirit, remind us to be tenderhearted and forgiving and to let the warmth of the light of Christ draw others to the Cross. In Jesus's name, amen.

Merry-Go-Round of Deceit

On the playground at my elementary school some years … okay, some decades ago was a flat, saucer-shaped, merry-go-round. It was the "Cujo" of merry-go-rounds and the most frightening piece of recreational equipment on the schoolyard. Capable of spinning at Mach 2 speeds, I avoided even coming near it, let alone attempting to ride it. I swore an evil groan announced every insidious rotation.

Peer pressure, however, starts at a very young age, enticing you into things you would not normally do. A few of the bold and beautiful finally convinced the young and restless (like me) into riding, all the while promising me that they "wouldn't go too fast." Uh-huh!

They, of course, spun me much faster than I wanted to go. For a short time, I tried to pretend I was enjoying the ride, working desperately to wear a smile, but then my stomach began to churn. I wanted off, but the ride was moving much too fast and my cries went unnoticed—or perhaps even ignored.

You know that feeling when your outsides do not match your insides; the moment you recognize the difficulty in trying to maintain a smile when all you really want to do is cry...or scream...or even lose your lunch! Your cries for mercy are either not heard or simply go unnoticed.

At some point in our lives, each of us has reaped the consequences of wrong choices, some of which can lead into sinful behavior. The smooth and seductive voice of sin always promises to take care of you but in the end, it spins you faster and longer than you initially intended.

There is an old saying that goes, "Sin always takes you farther than you want to go, keeps you longer than you want to stay, and costs you more than you are willing to pay."

Galatians 6:7–8 says, "Do not be deceived: God cannot be mocked. A man reaps what he sows. The one who sows to please his sinful nature...will reap destruction."

When we think that we are somehow immune to the consequences of sin or that possibly we will reap something different from what we've sown, we not only deceive ourselves but are also mocking God. The words of the Prophet Jeremiah tell us, "The heart is deceitful above all things and beyond cure" (Jeremiah 17:9).

Truly bright, intelligent, and even spiritual people are as susceptible to self-deception as the uneducated or spiritually lost, sometimes even more. Thicker portfolios often offer not only more alibis but scapegoats as well.

It is easy to blame others when sin is exposed, even claiming we had *no other choice.* The word of God says, "I have set before you life and death, the blessing and the curse. So choose life in order that you may live, you and your descendants" (Deut. 30:19).

Paul continues from Galatians 6:8, saying, "But the one who sows to the Spirit … shall reap eternal life." Our decisions ultimately determine our destiny. Sow a thought, reap an act; actions turn into habits; habits develop our character; character determines destiny.

Sin always begins as an enjoyable ride of pleasure, power, or fulfillment but ultimately results in a harvest of destruction: a destruction of relationships with others, as well as with God.

I definitely spent more years than I care to admit in God's preparatory school. However, regardless of all the foolish choices in my life, the moment I surrendered to God was the moment He turned things around for my good. Though God has not always eliminated every consequence, He has enabled me to use the years of rebellion as a tool of ministry to others, demonstrating the love, forgiveness, and mercy of God.

God is patient, loving, and kind no matter how long you've spent going around and around on the same old ride of habitual sin. It does not lessen God's love for you; it just may take you a little longer to get your footing.

Father, we thank you for Your righteousness, which enables us to walk in holiness before You. Thank you also that You accompany us even in our restlessness until we find our place in You. You chasten those whom You love to bring about Your perfect will in our lives. Forgetting the wasted time behind us, Father, we choose now to press on toward the mark of Your higher calling. In Jesus's name, amen.

Manifold Blessing

One of my favorite meals is old-fashioned chicken and noodles, preferably with the "thick" noodles. It was top on the list of family favorites as a child. One evening, heaven came down and glory filled our bellies when Mom served not only chicken and noodles but also mashed potatoes and corn as well... all in one meal! A volcano of carbohydrates, it was the manifold blessing of comfort foods, providing a quick surge of carbohydrate energy, later followed by a long nap on the sofa.

If you have never read the book of Jude, I encourage you to do so. It is not much longer than one of my columns, and I love the way he opens his letter. "Jude, a bond-servant of Jesus Christ, and brother of James, to those who are the called, beloved in God the Father, and kept for Jesus Christ: May mercy and peace and love be multiplied to you" (Jude 1:1–2).

Just as Apostle Paul proclaimed himself as a bondservant of Christ, Jude also introduces himself as such. He then dispenses the manifold blessing of mercy, peace, and love to the church. He initially had planned a different message but changed his mind in order to deal with a matter he felt was more urgent.

"Beloved, while I was making every effort to write you about our common salvation, I felt the necessity to write to you appealing that you contend earnestly for the faith which was once for all delivered to the saints" (Jude 1:3).

Jude's urgent concern was that certain persons had crept into the church, modifying the grace of God in an attempt to reinforce their decadent lifestyles, completely denying Jesus Christ as master and Lord. False believers among true Christians are what Jesus calls "tares" in the wheat. Jude called them "clouds without water" and "autumn trees without fruit."

The more things change, the more things stay the same. The corruption and hypocrisy in which the first-century church struggled has found its way into the twenty-first century church. Professing without possessing, many counterfeit and hollow leaders, as well as their members attempt to hide behind a veil of pious religiosity, giving cause for many to reject the church. God, however, is even more angered by our hypocrisy than we are, and He is the final Judge.

Jude's cautionary words do not instruct true believers to submerge themselves in their religious hidey-holes but rather to immerse themselves in the love of God. They were to encourage one another in their faith, remaining in a spirit of fervent prayer in order to carry out Jude's next challenge.

"And have mercy on some who are doubting; save others, snatching them out of the fire; and on some have mercy with fear, hating even the garment polluted by the flesh" (Jude 1:22–23).

The manifold blessing of mercy, peace, and love is available to every believer. "God, being rich in mercy... made us alive together with Christ... in order that in the ages to come He might show the surpassing riches of His grace in Jesus Christ" (Ephesians 2:4–7).

Through God's mercy, we are living examples of the grace of Jesus Christ, called to dispense mercy, peace, and love to an ungodly world. If we accept the manifold blessings of God, we must also be willing to accept the responsibilities of the true believer.

In these turbulent times, it is increasingly necessary for the church to contend earnestly for their faith. Jesus invites us to walk and work with Him in this world of confusing philosophies. I urge you, therefore, to spend time with one another, building one another up in your most holy faith. There is no better energizer than an enthusiastic discussion between passionate believers to revitalize the call of God on your life.

Beloved of God, may mercy, peace, and love be multiplied to you, bringing comfort as well as energy to your soul.

"Now to Him who is able to keep you from stumbling, and to make you stand in the presence of His glory blameless with great joy, to the only God our Savior, through Jesus Christ our Lord, be glory, majesty, dominion and authority, before all time and now and forever. Amen" (Jude 1:24–25).

Put Me in Coach

Junior high softball caused me to break into a sweat, though not from exertion but from the fear of someone hitting the ball in my direction. I am quite certain I played outfield for a very good reason.

I remember, as well, trying to fade into the background while seated on the bench as the basketball coach paced the floor directly in front of me, looking over prospective players. Though I was suited up, I was not really "in the game." I liked sports; I just liked them better from the bench or bleachers.

In sports, there are three types of participants: the active player; the suited, yet passive player (like me), and of course, the ever-present sideline observer. The active player eats and sleeps sports. He or she knows the rulebook inside and out and prepares both mentally and physically for the next game, days in advance. The active players surround themselves with likeminded people, and their motto is "No guts, no glory."

The passive player shows up for most practices, though he never really strives to learn all the plays but instead relies heavily on the knowledge of the serious players. On game day, one good excuse is reason enough to stay home. Then there are the sideline observers. These can be great cheerleaders but just as easily can become the most severe critics.

Have you ever noticed that when it comes to our personal faith, there are similar comparisons among believers? The active players on the field of faith are those who talk the talk and walk the walk. They know Scripture forward and backward and spend a great deal of time in their spiritual disciplines. They prepare for Sunday worship long before Sunday comes, and purposely surround themselves with other believers who can build up their faith.

The passive participants are those who love to wear the faith uniform, but Bible study is much too tiresome and demanding. They know just enough Scripture to be dangerous, and rely heavily on the faith of the more serious follower. On Sunday, one good excuse is all that is necessary to stay home.

The distant observers decided long ago that it was easier and safer to remain simply the observer. They are moved emotionally by the testimonies of the active players, secretly wishing they too could taste of the glory and joy that the faithful experience but fear their clumsy past disqualifies them from participating.

When it comes to following Christ completely, many know what they need to do but oftentimes lack the courage or confidence to do so. Surrender is never easy, but without it, it is impossible to follow wholeheartedly. No guts, no glory!

Many begin each new year with worn-out resolutions from the previous year. But what if your resolution is simply to get serious in your relationship with God? If you are one who has only warmed the spiritual bench or viewed spiritual things from the bleachers, it is your time to "get in the game."

As Paul said, "I do all things for the sake of the gospel, that I may become a fellow partaker of it. Do you not know that those who run in a race all run, but only one receives the prize? Run in such a way that you may win" (1 Corinthians 9: 23–24).

Let us mirror Paul's resolve with, "I count all things to be loss in view of the surpassing value of knowing Christ Jesus my Lord" (Philippians 3:8). "One thing I do: forgetting what lies behind and reaching forward to what lies ahead" (Philippians 3:13).

If you are one of the "active players," stay true to the mental, physical, and spiritual disciplines that have helped to strengthen you in your walk, seeking guidance and direction often from the rulebook of life—the Holy Bible. Demonstrate a faithful and obedient walk as an example to others. Press on for the sake of the gospel.

There is no greater reward in life than to know Christ wholly and to enjoy Him completely every day. Beloved, let His mercy and love lead you to true repentance unto an enduring and unshakable faith, while His goodness and kindness continually draw you closer to His side. Draw near to God, and He will draw near to you, for you are dearly loved.

Thank you, Father, that You supply all our needs according to Your riches in glory in Christ Jesus. In these troubling times, Lord, we need boldness more than ever. Strengthen us with all power, by Your spirit in the inner man, so that Christ will dwell in our hearts through faith that we may walk in the likeness of Christ. In Jesus's name, amen.

Divine Confines

Student driving was the height of my high school sophomore driver's education course. Time behind the actual wheel was the cherry atop the hours spent in the classroom memorizing rules, regulations, and road signs. With the majority of the class being farm kids, most considered themselves expert drivers already.

My shining moment came in the form of a question during my turn at the wheel. Driving down the highway, I approached a vehicle from behind traveling just under the speed limit, which, in 1975, was only fifty-five mph. With a shoe full of confidence and three years of dirt road experience, I arrogantly asked the instructor, "Can I pass this guy?"

Showing only a slight grin and a look of "I wish I had a dollar for every time I've heard that," he replied, "Sure, if you can do it without breaking the speed limit." Of course, I knew I could not, and I reluctantly pulled back, feeling utterly brainless for even asking the question.

Traffic laws, like moral laws, exist not only for our protection but also for peace and order on or off the road. For the obedient, they offer an element of security and safety, but for the defiant, they are a source of irritation. Even Scripture tells us that the law is not made for a righteous man but for the lawless and insubordinate.

"But we know that the Law is good, if one used it lawfully, realizing in fact that law is not made for a righteous man, but for those who are lawless and rebellious"(1 Timothy 1:8–9).

It seems as we add more and more manmade laws to our currently existing laws, the more lawlessness abounds. Laws that worked only a few years ago quickly become obsolete, leaving officials and politicians scrambling for even stricter revisions, while immorality lobbies for more tolerance.

President John Adams (1797–1801) said, "We have no government armed with power capable of contending with human passions unbridled by morality and religion. Our constitution was made only for a moral and religious people. It is wholly inadequate to the government of any other."

Jesus's words recorded in Luke 16:17 say, "It is easier for heaven and earth to pass away than for one stroke of a letter of the Law to fail." Psalms 19:7–11 tells us, "The law of the Lord is perfect, restoring the soul ... in keeping them there is great reward."

Manmade laws self-destruct over time and lead

only to future lawlessness because they fail to address the condition of the heart, the place where lawlessness breeds. Jesus addressed this when asked by a lawyer which of God's laws He felt was the greatest (Matthew 22:36).

Jesus summed up the whole law with two commandments: "You shall love the Lord your God with all your heart, with all your soul, and with all your mind ... you shall love your neighbor as yourself. The entire Law and the Prophets hang on these two commandments" (Matt 22:37–40).

Just like my eagerness to get around that seemingly slow driver, there have been times I thought God was moving a little too slowly, and I sought to "pass" Him to get what I wanted out of life. I wish I could say I pulled back, but instead I ignored His laws and principles, thinking I knew best for myself. God has a way of bringing you back to square one— and several times, if He has to.

There is a way that seems right to man but in its end is destruction. Every day, God sets before us life and death, blessings and curses. Today, take your foot off the accelerator and choose life that you, your family, your community, and our nation may live in the blessings of peace and security.

Father, Your law is perfect and cannot fail. Your judgments are true and righteous. Forgive us for giving into our sinful nature. Thank you that the law of the spirit of life in Christ sets us free from the law of sin and death. Through obedience and faith, we can enter into Your blessed rest. In Jesus's name, amen.

High Hopes

My feet were braced snuggly against the starting blocks, my fingers nudged as close to the yellow line as possible, and my right hand gripped the freshly taped baton. My heart pounded in my throat, and the tension in my legs was like that of the racehorse behind the starting gate.

I was the starter for the high school girls' 440 relay. We had an excellent team that year. I was a strong starter; the others were extremely powerful runners. Our team had drawn for the inside track in the fastest heat. We were positioned for triumph.

The instructions given by the coach with the starting gun were that there would be "no false starts." Jumping the gun resulted in immediate disqualification. No pressure!

"Runners, to your mark ... *get set ...* !"

And I'm sure you've guessed by now what happened. My overzealous legs overpowered my oxygen-deprived brain—and prematurely burst from the starting blocks! The whistle blew and my head pounded, as I knew I had just blown it for me ... and my team.

I guiltily looked around the track and watched as each red-and-blue-donned leg of our relay team dismally left their station. The toughest thing now that I had to do was meet them all in the middle of the field. If I could have dug a hole and buried myself, I would have.

Moments like this one have occurred for each of us at some time in our life. It may have had nothing to do with sports, but each of us has been, at some point, the target of ridicule, mockery, disappointment, anger, and even abandonment.

Perhaps it was the result of our own carelessness or disobedience, or maybe it was a result of someone else's neglect or abuse. Regardless, it leaves one feeling shunned, shamed, disowned, wounded, and painfully lonely.

Human nature and self-preservation drive us into hiding to cover our wounds and shield ourselves from the onslaught of heartless attacks. But one cannot bury one's heart deep enough to avoid the blows of self-disappointment, self-degradation, and feelings of unworthiness.

Too often, our search for hope and a sense of worth are in the things of this world—fame, glory, approval, success, wealth, even happiness—and all will leave us stranded mid-field with nowhere left to run. We try to conceal our hurt and shame with a variety of methods: self-medicating with alcohol, drugs, relationships, and even work, all eventually abandoning or destroying the very thing we tried so desperately to protect, our heart, leaving us in a worse condition than before.

The author of Hebrews reminds us of the one who will never leave us or forsake us. "This hope we have as an anchor of the soul, a hope both sure and steadfast and one which enters within the veil, where Jesus has entered as a forerunner for us" (Hebrews 6:19–20). God heals the brokenhearted and binds up their wounds. He supports the afflicted and brings down the wicked. The Lord's favor is upon those who fear Him (Psalm 147).

Placing all of our hope, faith, or trust in people, places, or things will eventually leave us discouraged, disappointed, and disillusioned. Hoping in hope alone will even come up empty. We cannot *hope* we are a Christian; we cannot *hope* we go to heaven; hoping only in an image of Christ is also to hope in vain.

Our hope is to be in nothing less than the precious blood of Jesus Christ and His righteousness. When Christ truly *is* our hope, He rules and reigns in our soul and our life. It was God's will to make known to us what has remained a mystery in the past regarding the riches of the glory of God, which is "Christ in you, the hope of glory" (Colossians 1:27).

When Christ is our hope, we can give up our quest for significance and purpose and simply rest in His unchanging grace. Paul, when speaking of his thorn in the flesh, said, "And He has said to me, 'My grace is sufficient for you, for power is perfected in weakness.' Most gladly, therefore, I will rather boast about my weakness, that the power of Christ may dwell in me" (2 Corinthians 12:9).

"May the God of hope fill you with all joy and peace, as you trust in Him, that you may overflow with hope by the power of the Holy Spirit" (Romans 15:13).

"My hope is built on nothing less than Jesus's blood and righteousness. I dare not trust the sweetest frame, but wholly lean on Jesus's name. On Christ, the solid rock I stand. All other ground is sinking sand; all other ground is sinking sand" (Composer of "Solid Rock"—William B. Bradbury, 1816–1868). Amen.

The Complacency Zone

George Carlin once said, "Have you ever noticed that anyone driving slower than you is an idiot, and anyone driving faster than you is a maniac?" A point taken from this is that as long as we are all going the same speed, following the same set of rules, keeping up with the traffic, and not pulling any fancy stuff, then driving is easier, less complicated, and a lot less dangerous. Status quo works well on the highway, but not so much in the church.

In the 1970s, young and passionate Christians bore the not-so-complimentary label of "Jesus Freaks." I remember hearing about these young radicals as an early teen. In my ignorance, I also began to join the ranks, labeling a few of my own friends who appeared "a little too religious."

We looked at this group as if they were some sort

of alien-like, "out there" spiritual fanatics who had nothing else to do with their time. Getting excited about religion was like getting excited about algebra! We joked and we laughed, but something pierced deep inside me with every sarcastic remark.

After all, I attended church and youth group. I had "gone forward," been baptized, and took weekly communion. I knew the standard hymns and sometimes even got into a sermon. I knew exactly when to slap on the spiritual face and cued in on all the nods. I looked like everyone else but made *zero* impact in the kingdom.

Second Chronicles 16:9 says, "For the eyes of the Lord move to and fro throughout the earth, that He may strongly support those whose hearts are completely His."

I love that! God searches the earth and sifts through the appearance of religiosity into the depths of the heart for those who have fallen in love with the Savior and whose lives have been radically changed because of a deep relationship with the King of kings and Lord of lords. They've been radically saved!

So is this to say that there are different degrees of salvation? Not necessarily. It may be, however, evidence of different levels of our love, obedience, and devotion, possibly even an important indicator of the validity of our salvation experience. We must not confuse *religion* and *relationship*.

In the church, we can sometimes get upset with those who go slower than the rest, the Sunday drivers, so to speak. On the other hand, we tend to become irritated or even intimidated by those who seem to have a little too much "get up and go" or perhaps dare to try something new. Tradition and status quo keeps things comfortable and safe. But even Jesus did not follow the status quo. Jesus lived dangerously!

Living dangerously is not to live recklessly but righteously, taking a stand for all that is good and just. Righteous motives always seek to protect and defend, discerning the chaotic surroundings through the light of God's Word. Selfish motives seek only their own way, with little regard for those around them, often leaving a trail of wreckage and debris in their wake.

Each one moves at his or her individual pace as the faith process unfolds in their lives. We cannot pressure anyone into "speeding up," nor should we ever attempt to "slow them down." Again, we should check our motives. We are to encourage and inspire one another, leading them through and around the potholes of life. Fueled by the grace of God and guided by His spirit, truth, and love. God's radical grace for us should compel us to live a life of radical obedience and devotion for Him!

If Sunday morning feels more like an empty exercise, and you feel as though you are just going through repetitive religious motions, you could be in danger of slipping into the *complacency zone*. It may be time to step out and live dangerously in the hand of God.

Lord of Glory, we thank you for Your radical example of love, sacrifice, and grace. Help us to shake off the dust of complacency and religiosity. I pray when Your roaming eyes move across our hearts that they would find us faithful and fully devoted to You, and that we may have the support of heaven and earth. In Jesus's name, amen.

My Sheep Hear My Voice

Nothing is more fearful as a child than to lose track of a parent while shopping in a large grocery store. Nothing is more comforting to a lost child than the distinct sound of their parent's voice.

I lost track of my mother once in what I thought at the time was a very large grocery store. Colorful cereal boxes with a "prize inside" sidetracked my attention for only a few short moments. Suddenly, panic rushed through my veins and I began the anxious pursuit, racing up and down and across the aisles of supermarket tile, dodging shopping carts and grocery displays in my path. My feet kept timely rhythm with my heart as I sprinted frantically through the store, trying desperately not to appear in distress.

Then I heard it—the voice that could still the stormy waters of grievances, part a sea of would-be troublemakers, and calm the fears of bedtime shadows—my mother's voice. She was calling my name. Like radar through dense fog, I amplified my auditory antennas, easily navigating my course back to her side, all because I recognized my mother's voice.

It was during a time of festival when Jesus walked into the entrance of the temple of Solomon. Some there pressed Jesus to reveal Himself saying, "How long will you keep us in suspense? If you are the Christ, tell us plainly" (John 10:24).

Jesus answered them and said, "I told you, and you do not believe; the works that I do ... testify of Me. But you do not believe because you are not my sheep. My sheep hear My voice and I know them and they follow Me" (John 10:27).

Jesus was saying that His sheep are those who hear [and recognize] His voice by faith, are known by Him, and from a servant's heart, lovingly keep His commandments. He then offers three promises in the next verse. He says, "And I give eternal life to them, and they shall never perish; and no one is able to snatch them out of My hand" (John 10:28).

Those who do not believe are not His sheep and therefore will not hear or distinguish His voice. Sadly, even many believers struggle in hearing and recognizing His voice in daily activities, perhaps amid the clutter of religious routine and tradition. It also can be difficult to hear His voice through the echo of past sin and failure.

"Be anxious for nothing, but in everything by prayer and supplication with thanksgiving let your requests be made known to God. And the peace of

God, which surpasses all comprehension, shall guard your hearts and your minds in Christ Jesus" (Phil. 4:6–7).

The life of the child of God can be reminiscent of our childhood days as we navigate through the aisles of worldly temptations. At times, we find ourselves captivated by the bright colors, flashing lights and promises of "hidden prizes". Suddenly, we recognize that we are on our own, lost and confused. Our panic, however, should cause us to run in an anxious pursuit toward God, listening attentively for His voice.

I've heard it said, "If you don't feel close to God, guess who moved." God in His love, grace, and mercy will never leave us or forsake us. Spending time with Him and in His Word sharpens your hearing and perks up your spiritual antenna, enabling you to hear His voice even more clearly. Listen! He's calling your name.

Father God, Your Word tells us that faith cometh by hearing, and hearing by the word of God. Your Word is the key that unlocks the doors of faith. Thank you, Lord, that as we hear Your voice and keep Your commandments, You bless us with the security of salvation and eternal life in You, and we can never be snatched from Your hand. Help us to be living testimonies of genuine and active faith. In Jesus's name, amen.

Keep It Simple

One of the joys I feel this younger generation missed out on is the thrill of churning homemade ice cream. Some of my favorite childhood memories are of sitting on the porch at Grandma's house, spinning the hand crank, taking turns with the other grandchildren as the cream-filled aluminum canister spun quickly through the icy salt water. With each turn of the arm, the cream, sugar and egg mixture became colder and thicker, as children and even adults grew increasingly anxious for the first scoop of the frozen delight.

With the advent of ice cream chain stores, simple homemade ice cream has become more a nostalgic treat reserved for holidays and special occasions. With so many flavors, including some that should not even be a flavor, choosing one can be a challenge for every ice cream enthusiast.

Though the methods of manufacturing ice cream have changed over time, the result has remained the same—a thick, creamy, frozen dessert suited for nearly every member of the ice cream lover's brigade. Except for the wide array of newfangled flavors and flavor enhancing additives, the main ingredients of cream, sugar, and eggs remain virtually untouched.

Since the days when Jesus walked the earth, the *delivery* of the message of the gospel has gone through its own forms of transformation. I once heard that early sound systems involved simply preaching from a boat launched out a slight distance in order to magnify the volume of the speaker's voice as it bounced off the surface of the water. We have come a long way.

As a child, I learned scores of Bible lessons from cardboard figurines in a three-by-four-foot sandbox. For today's children, computer Bible games and animated lessons have taken the place of the old sandbox. I still remember the foil-lined Nile with the baby Moses hidden in the bushes. And who can forget the flannel board?

"Jesus is the same yesterday, today, and forever" (Heb. 13:8). So too is the message of the gospel:

1. man is sinful
2. sin separates us from God
3. Christ died for our sin
4. salvation is a free gift
5. but we must receive it personally.

Nothing has changed about the message, except only for the *methods* of communicating that message.

It is sad when souls avoid receiving what God

has for them simply because they have decided in their mind that the gospel is complicated. They feel there are too many rules and regulations to learn, with things to do and promises to keep. Something in their past, perhaps even a church experience, drew them to conclude that religion just isn't for them. The truth is it's not about religion; it's about a relationship. Jesus Christ longs for a relationship.

When it comes to sharing the gospel, the greatest mistake we make as Christians is to think that someone else is better qualified in doing so. Part of what made churning ice cream so much fun as a child was the fact that it was a joint effort working toward a sweet reward. Ministry as well is a joint effort working toward a sweet reward. I love the scripture from 1 Corinthians 3:6, when Paul said, "I planted, Apollos watered, but it was God who was causing the growth." Sharing the gospel is a joint effort in the body of Christ, empowered by the Spirit of God.

Another mistake we make is to laden the gospel message with unnecessary additives, thinking it is too boring or uninteresting. Doing so distorts the truth of the message, drawing more attention to the additives rather than to the actual message, causing believers to seek out fancy flavors over foundational truth.

The message of the gospel is not "please visit our church so you can be saved here." The message of the gospel is simple, nothing added and nothing taken away. Like old-fashioned homemade ice cream, the gospel message is pure and simple. The sweet reward however, is the promise of eternal life.

"For God so loved the world that He gave His only begotten Son, that whosoever believes in Him, would not perish, but have everlasting life" (John 3:16).

The message was, and is, and always will be that God loves you and desires to give you abundant life on earth and eternal life in heaven. Just keep it simple!

Thank you, Father, for the work of the Holy Spirit in ministering to others. Forgive me of the times I have failed to share Your message with others who need to know You. Empower me by Your Spirit with words of faith, hope, and love, keeping the message simple and pure. Thank you for the gift of eternal life through Your Beloved Son. In Jesus's name, amen.

Tag, You're It!

I have written occasionally of what I thought were intimidating childhood schoolyard games primarily due to my size as a child. Tag, however, was one I excelled in since its basic requirements are speed and agility. I was small, wiry, and fast. Tag? No problem. Dodgeball? No way!

Of course, the object of Tag was for the person who was "it" to tag someone else while maintaining the established parameters of the game … if indeed there *were* parameters. It was not always obvious who exactly was "it," and latecomers to the game were easy prey for the enthusiastic player desirous of giving away their "it" status.

I always thought "it" was an odd name, wondering what exactly *it* was. It wasn't something you held in your hands or hid in your pocket. But once someone tagged you, you had *it* and you knew it. So did everyone else.

We can learn much from childhood games. Perhaps they are foundational for deeper significance later on, even in our Christian faith. If you think about it, Tag is a rudimentary evangelistic model that individuals, as well as churches, would do well in practicing.

Have you ever talked with someone who you knew had "it"? Have you ever been to a church that you knew had "it"? But what exactly is *it?* What is it that makes people get excited about their faith, and the mere mention of the name of Jesus brings a sparkle to their eyes? What is *it?*

What is it in some churches that you feel almost instantly upon entering? There is a palpable, almost tangible current of energy flowing through its members. It's more than just well orchestrated liturgy; the people there really love the Lord, and they love to worship.

Over a hundred years ago, Charles Spurgeon said, "To put new converts into most churches is like putting live chicks under a dead hen." Ouch! Sadly, his sentiments are still perfectly appropriate.

So what exactly is this thing that, when present, creates such enthusiasm, but such apathy when not? Is it genetics, talent, money, church membership, big screens, charismatic leaders? I'll give you a hint. Unless one is born again, he cannot see or experience *it.*

Jesus told Nicodemus, "The wind blows where it wishes and you hear the sound of it, but do not know where it comes from and where it is going; so is everyone who is born of the Spirit" (John 3:8).

Previously, Jesus replied to Nicodemus's question, saying, "Unless one is born again, he cannot see the kingdom of God ... and no one can enter [it] unless he is born of water and the Spirit" (John 3:3, 5). Romans 14:17 defines for us the kingdom of God: "For the kingdom of God is ... righteousness (through Christ) and peace (through Christ) and joy in the Holy Spirit" (parentheses mine).

Like the wind, you cannot see the kingdom of God, but *it* reveals itself in the broken and surrendered heart, the heart that is truly born again, born, not of the flesh or of church membership, but born of the Spirit. The spirit-filled, transparent individual with a deep passion for God, desiring to live continually in His presence with a zealous desire for the lost has *it*. The church filled with these individuals has *it*.

Jesus did not die so that we could become members of organized religion, wearing a badge of church membership and hosting weekly fundraisers. Jesus was crucified, dead and buried, and rose again that we might live in the righteousness of Christ, free of the torturous chains of our sin and full of unspeakable joy. We are to have a heart like His, the kind of heart that is burdened for the lost, desiring to heal the sick and wounded, all the while seeking to glorify the Father.

The good news is that unlike the game of Tag, size, speed, or talent is not necessarily required. There is no scorekeeping, and no one loses. There are no established parameters. It is a win-win situation. If someone tagged you one day with the love of Christ, it is now time for you to go tag another ... and another ... in Jesus's name.

Father, it is my prayer that we will become enthusiastic participants in "tagging" someone else with the love of Christ and that we would live our lives in such a way that people know we have *it*. Thank you for the righteousness of Christ, His peace, and joy in the Holy Spirit. In Jesus's name, amen.

Give Me Some Skin

I have learned that if you listen very carefully, you can hear God speaking through the lips of your little ones. There have been numerous times when the words of my young children brought conviction upon me as I hustled through the daily routines of the busy parent. God's Word tells us we are to have the faith of a child. I think that as adults we can learn much from our children if indeed we really listen.

One stormy evening many years ago, we were putting the children to bed. Our boys shared a room and went on to bed without incident. Our three-year-old daughter, however, was another story. She was already planning her strategy to sleep with us. She was not exactly pleasant bed company, as she usually ended up sleeping crosswise with her feet in someone's face.

I steered her back to her room and placed her back into her own bed. We visited for a few minutes and said another prayer. Before I left, I tried to reassure her of her safety, with all of her teddy bears tucked in tightly around her, and then reminded her that Jesus was always with her too.

Pining for the inevitable last word, she looked up at me from beneath her blankets and with the saddest of eyes said, "But I need somebody with *skin* on!"

So as she climbed into our bed (yes, she won that one), I lay there beside her and thought about the depth of the words she had just spoken. I realized that too many times in ministering to others we attempt to offer a quick fix with words of consolation and promises of God's presence.

There is a popular phrase among church leaders stating, "People don't care how much you know until they know how much you care." I have found this to be profoundly true. There are times when someone needs more than brief consolation; they need you! And isn't that what Jesus calls us to do?

Second Corinthians 1:3–4 declares, "Blessed be the God and Father of our Lord Jesus Christ, the Father of mercies, and the God of all comfort, who comforts us in all our afflictions, that we may be able to comfort those which are in any affliction, by the [same] comfort with which we ourselves are comforted of God."

God does not comfort us just to make us comfortable but to make us *comforters!*

I question the sometimes-flippant use of the adage "misery loves company." It can be inclined to suggest the notion that misery prefers *like* or *similar* company. If that is true, then misery will always be miserable. What misery really wants is help! It wants understanding, compassion, mercy, grace, forgiveness, and acceptance. It wants to be heard, and many times, it just wants to be held!

God is calling us to put into practice with others what He has done for us. Recognize that sometimes people need more than just a pat on the back; they need true, heartfelt comfort, full of mercy and compassion. It is the beauty of the family of God living out the kingdom of God.

Heavenly Father, I thank you for the times You speak to us through our little ones. Give us ears to hear and hearts to receive. Help us to comfort others with the same comfort by which we have been comforted. Teach us to be sensitive and compassionate. Teach us to be Jesus ... *with skin on!* In His precious name, amen.

Got Arrows?

Every father looks forward to the day when he is finally able to take his son along on the traditional "hunt." Sometimes the excursion becomes more of a valuable lesson than a successful hunt.

Early one morning, my husband, Chuck, readied our seven-year-old son, Cory, for this sacred tradition. I filled one thermos with hot chocolate, another with coffee, and waved as the mighty hunters set out for the wild kingdom of northern Grant County. It was bow season in Oklahoma, which adds a completely different element to the hunting experience.

All good hunters quickly learn that stealth and silence are crucial, and Cory received extensive instruction in this discipline. Equipped with bow-hunting gear, he and my husband quietly made their way through the wooded terrain, dried autumn leaves crunching beneath their leather boots.

Suddenly, with a gentle tug on the back of his

dad's jacket, the still of the moment was broken as Cory whispered, "D-a-ad."

Chuck turned and motioned "quiet" while continuing toward his usual hunting spot. Moments later, as my husband began to inspect the tree stand, Cory firmly tapped his dad on the back and again whispered, "But D-a-a-ad."

Chuck gave him the "just a minute" signal as he helped Cory up into the stand. With the strong-willed hunters finally settled in place, Cory attempted one last time, whispering loudly, "But D-a-a-ad!"

Chuck relented. "Cory, yes, what is it?"

Cory answered, "You forgot your arrows!"

There was a time when the bow and arrow were more than hunting gear; they were a necessity, a means of self-defense against the enemy. The good warrior was well trained for accuracy and made sure his quiver was well equipped with carefully sharpened arrows. A bow without arrows falls short of its intent. One is in need of the other.

Arrows in Scripture hold various representations, but for this particular narrative, arrows represent spiritual truths. As believers, we can see the necessity for taking care not only to gather but also to sharpen our arrows, whether we are speaking of spiritual warfare or simply the accurate application of the truth in a particular situation.

Second Timothy 3:17 says, "All scripture is inspired by God and profitable for teaching, for reproof, for correction, for training in righteousness;

so that the man (or woman) of God may be adequate, equipped for every good work."

Second Timothy 2:15 says, "Be diligent to present yourself approved to God as a workman [or warrior] who does not need to be ashamed, accurately handling the word of truth."

I have found myself—maybe you have too—in situations when I felt the Spirit urging me to minister a word or pray with someone, and panic raced through my body like a bolt of lightning. It is in those moments that we realize the importance of gathering truth through memorization of Scripture. We can only recall what we have attained through study. We sharpen our skills through consistent use of what we have learned.

It is essential for the Christian first to *know* the truth of God's Word, to gather it as precious arrows of a warrior, then to accurately and skillfully apply it in his or her life or in the lives of others. Just as the arrow requires a strong bow and a skilled archer, the arrows of truth are dependent upon the bold faith of the adequately prepared Christian for an incisive aim, in season … and even out of season.

Holy God, like a warrior draws arrows from his quiver, may we be diligent to prepare ourselves by Your Word so that we are able to reach into our memory quiver and pull out the proper words of truth, being ready at all times. We thank you for Your Word, Father. We are not ashamed of the gospel, for it is the power of God for salvation to all who believe. Hallelujah to the Lamb!

Freedom Fighters

When the kids were small, we took on a project of hatching quail eggs, raising them until old enough to release. We eagerly gained the use of an incubator and a few dozen very tiny quail eggs. Placing the box on a counter beneath a window, we positioned the special lamp over our new and crowded maternity ward. We then watched expectantly the following weeks for the first signs of life.

The miracle began one day as we noticed the eggs moving ever so slightly. Their movement reminded me of the dancing beans I had seen as a child. Excitement grew as we heard tiny tapping sounds from within the shell. This was the moment we had been waiting for!

Inexperienced with quail hatching as I was, I noticed one of the first eggs seemed to be in trouble. The tiny bird had pecked for what seemed a very long time but was not making as much progress as I thought he should. It was obvious he needed my help!

So with the assistance of a sewing needle and the precision of a surgeon, I picked up the fragile egg and very delicately began to remove tiny portions of the stubborn shell that seemed to be in the way. I chipped enough away to ensure a quick and painless entry, laid the egg back down, and left the infant quail to do the rest, feeling rather heroic in my rescue.

A few hours later, I returned to the quail nursery and to my shock and disbelief, my "free bird" was barely alive. By the next day, he was dead. I learned later that the very process of pecking through the shell is a sometimes lengthy but necessary task for the young chicks in order to gain strength, stamina, and maturity. I had robbed the baby quail of the opportunity to become what nature had intended, and I unwittingly killed him.

It is natural for us to want to come to the aid of one who is in trouble. As Christians, God calls us to come alongside our brother or sister in Christ as well as those who have yet to make His acquaintance. I have found myself at times wanting to do as I did with the quail egg and, through impatience, apply a little too much "encouragement" in their journey. I forget that the struggle is necessary.

Our journey toward and with God is as unique and individual as we are. The struggles and challenges we bear build strength and character. To deny someone of that struggle short-circuits unique opportunities. Painful as it seems, it is wise to step back and allow God's will to unfold in the appointed time.

Unlike my "project free bird" calamity, God is ever patient. He will bless even the blunders of the overzealous freedom fighters in their attempts to minister truth into the life of another. While man's love often disappoints, God's love never fails.

First Corinthians 7:17 reminds us that, "Only, as the Lord has assigned to each one, as God has called each, in this manner let him walk." Remember also "where the Spirit of the Lord is, there is liberty" (2 Corinthians 3:17).

There are no quick and painless journeys through life in the kingdom of God. There also are no drag marks to the foot of the cross. There are lessons to learn and breakthroughs to make. We grow; we mature; we gain wisdom, insight, and understanding, compelling us to the next level from glory to glory!

Blessed be the God and Father of our Lord Jesus Christ. Thank you, Lord for every opportunity that brings us closer to You. Be glorified, Father, even in our blunders as we minister in spirit and in truth. May the blind be made to see and the bound be set free in Jesus's name. For whom the Son sets free is free indeed! Hallelujah to our King.

People Get Ready

My husband is a list maker. He makes a daily list for nearly everything he does. I used to tease him about his obsession but decided later that he may be on to something. Our middle son, Cole, picked up the same organizing traits; however, he started at a much younger age. During his elementary years, Cole was diligent to lay his school clothes out at night to prepare for the next morning; something many people do ... right?

The difference was he *laid* all his clothes completely out on the floor, beginning with the shirt (sleeves out), tucked into the pants (with belt), socks resting comfortably inside the shoes that were carefully placed at the hem of the jeans. It literally looked as if he had been *raptured* straight out of his clothing while lying face-up on the floor.

Comical as it was, my son never had to search for clothes or shoes on a school morning; and my husband seldom forgets a meeting or an appointment. I surely cannot say that about myself. Item-izing plans and being diligent to write them down and carry them out demonstrates focus, purpose, and preparedness.

We spend much of our time in preparation. We prepare and plan for weddings, graduations, college, new homes, and occasionally, even children. We also prepare for disasters that may or may not occur with insurance for our health, our cars, our homes, and a host of other items. The meteorologist prepares us for approaching storms days in advance.

Readiness demands preparation. You cannot have one without the other. The benefit of prepara-tion is readiness; readiness generates security; secu-rity offers rest.

We typically understand readiness as preparing oneself mentally or physically for an event or experi-ence. But what about things of a spiritual nature? We must ask ourselves, "What of my eternal future? Am I ready spiritually? Have I prepared my family and my children?"

Jesus's parable of the ten virgins (in Matt. 25:1-13) demonstrates preparation and readiness. Of the ten virgins invited to the wedding, five were wise and five were foolish. The wise virgins took extra oil for their lamps in preparation for the arrival of the bridegroom should he be delayed. The parable con-veyed that the bridegroom arrived while the foolish virgins had gone to buy more oil, and only the wise virgins, who had come prepared, were allowed into the wedding.

Jesus said, "Those who were ready went in with him to the wedding; and the door was shut" (Matthew 25:10). And as for the five who rushed out to buy oil at the last minute, they returned to a closed door and a missed opportunity.

Each of us is given a lifetime to prepare spiritually for our future. The trouble is that no one knows exactly what a lifetime is for each person. It could be years from now for some; days, or months for others. No one knows the number of days each one is given. Therefore the time to prepare for eternity is now. God's favor is available today; today is the day of salvation.

"Behold, now is 'the acceptable time,' behold, now is 'the day of salvation'" (2 Corinthians 6:2, Isaiah 49:8).

Father in heaven, I thank you for the gift of salvation through Jesus Christ, Your Son. Stir the hearts of those who are in spiritual slumber. Deliver them out of the stronghold of unbelief. Remind us, Father, it is not enough simply to know about You; but with our hearts, we must believe and receive Your gift of salvation. Make ready a people prepared for the Lord, for when our soul is secure, we find our rest in You. In Jesus's name, amen.

Gift of Adoption

One afternoon, a twelve-year-old boy came to the house to see the kids. My boys weren't home at the time, so I invited him into the living room to wait for them. He slumped onto the couch, threw his arms behind his head, and said, "Man, I've never been so bummed out."

Concerned, I sat down next to him to see if he would continue, and I waited.

He finally added, "I just found out I was adopted."

I have to admit it hit me like a ton of bricks as well, but I was a bit anxious now with what to say. What do you tell a child who has made such an earth-shattering discovery? I had no experience with issues of adoption. I wasn't sure I even knew anyone who was adopted.

After pausing to collect my thoughts, I finally said, "Well, you know, I think you must have been awfully special for them to have chosen you. What a blessing you must be."

I don't know whether that was the right thing to say or not. He never said much afterward. I think he eventually made peace with his discovery and accepted his adoption. He grew to be a very fine young man as well as an extremely talented musician.

We are born into this world as children of God, created by God. However, the fall of man created an estrangement in our relationship to our heavenly Father. It is a simple fact; *sin* separates us from a holy God.

The blood of Christ changes our status from God's creation to sons and daughters of God, joint-heirs with Christ, and true children of God. Christ enables us to now cry out, "Abba, Father," Abba being an Aramaic word equivalent to our word *daddy*. It can also be translated, "Father, dear Father."

"God sent forth His Son...in order that He might redeem us...that we might receive the adoption as sons. And because you are sons, God has sent forth the Spirit of His Son into our hearts, crying, 'Abba, Father!'" (Galatians 4:4–6).

Ephesians 1:5 tells us, "In love He predestined us to adoption as sons through Jesus Christ to Himself, according to the kind intention of His will."

I love that—"the kind intention of His will." God intends love, acceptance, holiness, and blamelessness for us. The Father has not left us as orphans to make it on our own but has provided a way of adoption unto Him through Jesus Christ. When we accept and receive the gift of adoption from our heavenly Father through Jesus, we become children of the King—joint-heirs with Christ!

God chose us from the foundation of the world. We will either accept or refuse the prearranged adoption into the family of God. Refusing the gift will leave us on our own, ultimately leading to destruction.

Sin will always leave us as orphans feeling lost and confused, abandoned and homeless. It will leave us to pick up the shattered pieces of our lives as the bony finger of fear and accusation ruthlessly points to the regrets of our past, the condition of the present, and the hopelessness of our future.

But hallelujah, God knows the thoughts and plans He has for our future, one of joy, peace, and righteousness. What a blessing to be chosen by Almighty God. What an honor to call him Abba, Father.

Father God, holy and righteous, we bow before Your throne to thank You for Your great mercy and for the gift of adoption. Thank you for choosing us even before we were formed in our mother's womb. As we accept Your will for our lives, we also receive the grace and mercy provided to us through Jesus Christ. We are now children of the King! Glory to the Lamb of God!

What's Your Flavor?

Several years ago, I assisted my daughter with her fourth-grade science project. She decided upon presenting a comparison in the flavors of two competing cola drinks to see if people could really tell the difference. We labeled them "Cola A" and "Cola B."

Putting the rubber to the road, we rigged up the little red wagon with an ice chest containing our secretly disguised contestants, furnished bathroom-sized paper cups, and set off on "Project Top Pop" to survey residents in the nearest housing addition. Going house to house, we polled men and women of all ages, performing the sniff test then the taste test, carefully noting their responses on a demographic chart.

The conclusion of our poll revealed that many who thought they could tell the difference between the two were surprised to discover they could not. There were a few die-hard "Cola A" drinkers and vice versa, who immediately detected the difference, but several also made this comment: "You know? It doesn't really matter. It's all pop!" We had fun, as did the neighbors who also received three delightful ounces of afternoon refreshment.

Though not a survey, I have found that when asked about their faith, a typical response of many is to name their denominational preference rather than simply saying, "I am a Christian." Maybe for some it seems a less provocative response; for others it may be a form of status to be a part of a particular church; but for whatever reason, it's between them and God.

It doesn't really matter what "flavor" you are, whether you sit quietly and meditate, jump and shout hallelujah, lift your hands in praise or sit on them. Where the rubber meets the road is the difference we are making among the people. Are lives being changed? Are families being restored? Are the shackles of sin falling off? *Are we proclaiming Christ?*

I confess that early in my faith journey I was a very closed-minded, die-hard Pharisaical pew sitter. I questioned the intentions of nearly every television evangelist or anyone who lifted their hands or shouted "Amen" in the middle of the service. I felt it surely was for show or selfish ambition. The fact is that for some it very well could have been; for others, it was not, but what is that to me?

Paul reminded the believers of Philippi that in his absence they would likely come across two types of preachers, those who proclaim Christ out of love and others who proclaim Christ out of selfish ambition.

> Some, to be sure, are preaching Christ even from envy and strife, but some also from good will; the latter do it out of love, knowing that I am appointed for the defense of the gospel; the former proclaim Christ out of selfish ambition, rather than from pure motives, thinking to cause me distress in my imprisonment.
>
> Philippians 1:15–17

To paraphrase, he goes on to say something like, "So what? Get over it." (Okay, that's my translation!)

He says, "What then? Only that in every way, whether in pretense or in truth, Christ is proclaimed; and in this I rejoice, yes, and I will rejoice" (Philippians 1:18).

Time, maturity, and understanding opened my closed mind, allowing the freedom to worship as the Spirit leads. I also no longer consider all televangelists as frauds. One can receive sound principles and teaching from a number of televised ministries. You may be surprised to discover that their differences indeed prove to enrich your faith. I also learned that God even uses carnality to advance the kingdom, if He so chooses. (Matt. 1, James 2:25)

There will come a day when we stand before God, and the question He will ask will not be, "What denomination were you from?" Nor will it matter whether or not we approved of every messenger of Christ. No, the question will simply be, "What did you do with My Son?"

Holy God, maker of heaven and earth and keeper of my heart, thank you for the transforming power of Jesus Christ. May our worship to You, O God, be in spirit and in truth. Let our minds be fixed on Christ and not on our differences, for it is there that we will witness the power and glory of the Son of God! Amen.

Do You See What I See?

Today they are called retro trees, but in the sixties and early seventies, silver aluminum Christmas trees were quite the rave. Our family had one that was full and bushy, adorned with dark pink, shiny glass ornaments. My grandparents' aluminum tree was more slender but filled with royal blue satin ornaments beautifully displayed in the living room picture window.

Many years ago, when our kids were small, times became rather tough for several months. The eighties oil boom had gone bust while businesses and families struggled to make ends meet, including us. Christmastime was soon approaching, and my stomach began to ache knowing that the Christmas tree would not have as much under it that year.

Then it hit me—the Christmas tree! We had

always purchased live trees in the past and just did not feel as though we could afford one that year. My husband remembered going through old boxes of decorations belonging to his grandmother a few years before, including a box containing their old aluminum tree. I was excited at the thought of a nostalgic Christmas tree and relieved at not having to purchase one.

The moment arrived as my husband placed the old box in the center of the room, and the kids immediately began to pull the branches out of the crumbling paper sheaths. Enthusiasm soon turned to disappointment as we slowly began to erect what we later called "Charlie Brown's Aluminum Tree." The branches looked more like foil rods with a shiny wild frazzle on the end. We were hoping against hope the ornaments would miraculously fill in the huge gaps.

As we stood gazing at our Charlie Brown tree, tilting our heads first one way and then another, gloom began to overtake me. Then the words of my four-year-old son shook me from my trance: "If you do this, it looks really bushy!"

I turned to find him standing with his head tilting backward and his eyes squinting nearly shut. So I tried it. He was right! With the help of the overhead track lighting filtering through the eyelashes, the tree appeared full and bushy. It all depended on how you looked at it!

I wish I could say it turned out to be the best Christmas ever that year. Looking back, however, it is the Christmas I think of most often—not because of the emotional pain or the lack of gifts under the tree, but because of a greater lesson learned that day.

"Why do you hide yourself in times of trouble?" (Psalm 10:1 NIV). I am sure I have posed this question myself a time or two over the years. In fact, after going through trials, we discover that God never hides but was there all along. He Himself has said, "I will never leave you, nor forsake you" (Hebrews 13:5 ESV).

When allowed to go through the dark places, we begin to see light we did not know existed. Painful times can have a particular objective for us in that they bring us to the end of ourselves, enabling us to discover the treasure hidden in the darkness. It is there we find we have the ability to see through spiritual eyes to behold what we had missed all along.

Father, thank you for the gift of Your Son, that whosoever believes in Him would not perish but have eternal life in Christ Jesus. Lord, when times are tough and we feel that all hope is lost, help us to see with spiritual eyes as we direct our thoughts and prayers toward You. Lead us to others who are also in need of Your touch, and enable us to meet their needs. In Jesus's name, amen.

Help, I'm Talking!

It seems every young family has at least one Curious George with which to add a touch of interest to the most ordinary moments. One afternoon, my loquacious three-year-old son and I were out for a leisurely shop. I was expecting our second child in only a matter of weeks and decided to stop and rest my feet at the makeup counter of a downtown department store.

A much older woman who was, as my grandpa used to say, a little "fleshy," had taken the seat next to me preparing for a makeover. Curious George stood beside me, carefully looking her up and down, glancing back at my large, expectant belly.

"Are you gonna have a baby too?" he innocently asked her.

Fortunately, she was a kind, gentle, and extremely understanding woman. She chuckled warmly, bent over to look him in the eyes, and tenderly replied, "No, dear. I just have a round belly."

My expression surely begged forgiveness, but with smiling eyes and a wink, she soothingly nodded the look of "It's okay, Mom."

Children are not the only ones susceptible to saying the wrong things. We often find ourselves caught in moments of impromptu verbiage that is often embarrassing or even inadvertently insulting. There have been times I have detected that instant of persistent prattle, and I hear my inner voice screaming, "Help. I'm talking, and I can't shut up!"

What is it about anxiety, anticipation, or even those tense moments of dead air space that triggers the Chatty Cathy syndrome? Besides a little embarrassment, you may also find yourself making promises you didn't intend to make. Jesus reminds us to consider our words carefully when He said, "Let your 'Yes' be 'Yes' and your 'No', 'No'" (Matthew 5:37).

Proverbs 6:2 says, "You are snared with the words of your lips; you are caught by the speech of your mouth."

Proverbs 10:19 tells us, "In a multitude of words transgression is not lacking, but he who restrains his lips is prudent."

The book of Proverbs speaks often of the wisdom of "controlled speech" as well as the folly of a loose tongue, whether it be in the form of "too many words", angry speech, or even untimely words. "Like apples of gold in settings of silver is a word spoken in right circumstances" (Prov. 25:11).

Abraham Lincoln surely understood the words of Proverbs when he said, "Better to remain silent and be thought a fool, than to speak and remove all doubt."

We have witnessed politicians use a multitude of words to convey their message. It seems the rule of thumb is most often, "If you can't sway them with statistics, then vex them with vagueness!"

Wise or foolish, saved or lost, anyone can easily engage the mouth before the brain is in gear. We are human; it is going to happen. It is in those moments, however, that we consider the cross. Do I need to ask forgiveness for an untimely word or even unintentional hurtful remark?

I hope that with time and experience, and a little personal awareness, those unfortunate instances will become fewer rather than greater. Making Proverbs a part of our daily reading is most helpful in that process. Besides being some of the best adages, as well as humorous one-liners, they are a wealth of wisdom and knowledge for every age.

I have often heard that with two ears and one mouth, we need to listen twice as much as we speak and to speak slowly so the brain can keep up. Can we say the words of our mouth glorify God while pointing others to Christ? Are the words we speak like apples of gold?

Father, Your Word says that he that does not rule over his own spirit is like a city without walls. We recognize our need to exercise self-control in our lives, which is a fruit of the Spirit. Strengthen us by Your spirit, Lord. Thank you for Your precious fruit imparted to us, which enables us to practice a godly life of joy, peace, patience, kindness, goodness, faithfulness and gentleness, and self-control. In Jesus's name, amen.

Faith Invaders

Several years ago we lived in a modular-style home back dropped by a field of Oklahoma prairie grass, which we quickly discovered was the habitat of a host of troublesome tenants. Upon the first traces of our tiny intruders of the gray and whiskery kind, we armed ourselves with mousetraps and peanut butter then went to bed and waited, for behold, we knew not of the hour the mouse would return.

Within only minutes, my husband and I delighted in the sound of the trap snapping down on our "verminian" enemy. However, our victory dance ended abruptly.

Apparently, the trap had only come down upon the tail or a leg, as suddenly we heard the sound of the mouse racing back and forth at mach speed inside our bedroom's modular wall, trying desperately to free itself.

Then silence fell as he seemingly shed the trap, and now only the sound of scurrying little feet inside the wall held me hostage in my own bed. Our joy had turned into mourning, with weeping and wailing and gnashing of teeth.

We grew weary of the traps and eventually went throughout the entire house sealing off any likely entrances into the home as best we could. Even the smallest crack was an open invitation to future invaders. Finally, the furry felon infringements faded to fewer frequencies.

One of the most difficult disciplines for the growing Christian is that of guarding the heart and mind. We may be quick to keep out obvious influences contrary to the will or commandments of God, but we can easily miss the little things. Tiny cracks in our defense will allow old thoughts, old habits, fear, worldly wisdom, and a host of other minor nuisances, which in time can lead to a major infestation of spiritual doubt and distrust, holding us hostage to our past, rendering us ineffective in our faith.

The Apostle Paul charged Timothy to guard himself from the influence of the world, to be an example of true godliness. He urged him to "constantly be nourished on the words of faith ... and discipline yourself for the purpose of godliness; for bodily discipline is only of little profit, but godliness is profitable for *all* things, since it holds promise for the present life and for the life to come" (1 Timothy 4:6–8).

Paul had also instructed the church in Rome to "not be conformed to this world, but be transformed by the renewing of your mind" (Romans 12:2). Renewing of the mind comes not through salvation alone but through the washing of the word of God on a daily basis, along with the practice of prayer. Do not worry about the body. The body will do what mind tells it to do. The mind bathed in the word and in prayer will naturally lean toward godliness.

So where are the "tiny cracks"? Most times, it's called life. Life's interruptions creep in unexpectedly, gnawing away at your prayer time, your devotions or time spent in the Word. It leaves its tracks of irritability, impatience, bitterness, or discontent. A discerning spirit will quickly recognize the "tracks" and return swiftly to the throne of grace, where the peace of God will guard your heart and mind in Christ Jesus.

Sealing up the tiny cracks in our house was time consuming, but it was necessary. The same is true for the serious Christian desiring true godliness. Prayer, Bible reading, Bible study and scripture memory do take time, but are critical to our spiritual health and growth. They are disciplines that lead to a fuller life and a deeper walk with Christ.

Father, I thank You for equipping us with every good thing. Your Word reminds us to let our minds dwell on things that are true, honorable, and right. Grant us spiritual discernment to distinguish and remedy the tiny cracks in our faith that would attempt to hinder our walk with You. In Jesus's name, amen.

Sweet Hour of Prayer

Nothing is more precious than a simple prayer coming from the tender lips of a small child. Several years ago, as we sat down to dinner, our four-year-old daughter informed everyone (rather emphatically) it was her turn to say the blessing over our meal. Her father and I felt that familiar heart tug at the boldness of her young faith.

Her brothers, however, assumed the proverbial "this oughta be good" posture. So with hands folded and heads bowed (and one final check to make sure everyone was following the rules), she began her sweet prayer. Instead of the typical mealtime "God is great, God is good" prayer, she wanted to recite the newly memorized "Lord's Prayer."

"Our Fotter, who awt in heaven, howdid be Dy

name. Dy kingdom come, Dy will be done, on erf as it is in heaven…"

She continued with one eye peeled (and obviously, I did too). She was eyeing her older brother who loved to antagonize, and who was mouthing the prayer with excessive animation, mocking her mercilessly. She was trying her best to control herself long enough to finish the prayer, but I could tell the fire was building, and she was getting a little louder and a little more… oh, shall we say *fervent* as she neared the end of her prayer.

She quickly rattled off, "For dine is da kingdom and da power and da glowy forever…*AMEN!*"

Before we could even raise our heads, I saw the blur of a tiny arm in motion as she swung at her brother, popping him across the shoulder. Ah, it's those precious moments in the wonder years that, as they say, we can laugh about now.

We all have had those moments when our prayers are a little "preoccupied" or "distracted." Our adversary, the devil, will mock us in our attempts, making us believe our prayers are worthless, silly, or that God has things of more importance at His attention.

Psalm 109:4 declares, "In return for my love, they act as my accusers, but I am in prayer." In this passage, David's adversaries hate him without reason, returning David's love for them with hatred. David struggled against the pain his accusers caused, but rather than retaliate, he resorted to prayer. The more they mocked, the more he prayed.

First Thessalonians 5:17 reminds us to "pray

without ceasing." While we can't possibly stay in prayer every minute of the day, we can stay in an attitude of prayer in continuous communion with God. Too often, we give up praying before seeing the manifestations of our prayer. If you believe the Lord for something, then do not cease praying until the answer comes.

"Therefore I tell you, whatever you ask for in prayer, believe that you have received it, and it will be yours" (Mark 11:24).

God knows the true intentions of our hearts. He knows what we need even before we ask. Giving voice to our requests helps to confirm our faith, encourage our hearts, and deepen our relationship with God. Work to develop your personal prayer life through methods that work for you, your schedule, and your habits. Furthermore, be aware of those things that can easily distract, being thankful always that we have access to the throne room of grace through simple and private prayer.

"Devote yourselves to prayer, keeping alert in it with an attitude of thanksgiving" (Col. 4:2).

"Rejoice always; pray without ceasing; in everything give thanks; for this is God's will for you in Christ Jesus" (1 Thess. 5:16, 17, 18).

Thank you, Father, that You hearken to the tiniest of prayers, and that we may come boldly to Your throne of grace. Even when we do not know what or how to pray, Your Word tells us that the Spirit makes intercession for us with groanings that cannot be uttered. We praise You, God, for the kingdom and the power and the glory is Yours forever and ever. Amen.

Classroom of Grace

My young daughter beamed with excitement the day she started kindergarten. She had anxiously watched her brothers in the past as they packed their backpacks for school and had been chattering incessantly about "her school" for days. Donning her new pink backpack, she was ready to go ... or so we thought.

She pounced out of bed that first morning, happily went to school, and returned from school all smiles and full of stories. *This is good,* I thought. The next morning, however, I woke her and cheerfully whispered, "It's time for school" then proceeded to finish breakfast. Not quite as excited as the previous morning, with heavy feet she trudged into the kitchen, blanket in tow, fell to the floor in her pajamas, and wailed, "You mean we have to do this *every day?*"

"Yes, child," I replied, "for at least the next thirteen years."

As it turned out, after only a few days, we agreed

with the teacher that she was not quite ready for kindergarten. With a summer birthday, we decided to give her one more year at home, which turned out to be the appropriate decision.

Just as there is proper timing for our education, there is also proper timing in our spiritual growth. We gradually move through the mathematics, language, science, music, and PE training of God's economy. Attempting to force any of it too early can end in frustration and disappointment.

Let us review a quick refresher course of the basics.

Mathematics, according to the Apostle Paul, is "one plus one equals one." First Corinthians 6:17 says, "But the one who joins himself to the Lord is one spirit with Him." When we receive Him by faith, we are joined in spirit with Christ. You plus anything else will fall short of the answer to any of your problems.

Next stop: Language 101—God speaks to us often; the challenge is in understanding what He is saying. Malcomb Muggeridge is worth repeating: "Every happening great and small is a parable whereby God speaks to us, and the art of life is to get the message." All of heaven and earth declare of His glory, and His sheep hear His voice.

On to Science class—Humanism and Darwinism have deceived many with the theory of no divine authority. "The fool says in his heart, 'There is no God'" (Psalm 14:1 NIV). God's Word declares,

He spreads out the northern skies over empty space; He suspends the earth over nothing ... He marks out the horizon on the face of the waters for a boundary between light and darkness. By His power He churned up the sea; by His breath the skies became fair; and these are but the outer fringes of His works; how faint the whisper we hear of Him! Who then can understand the thunder of His power?

Job 26:7–14 NIV

I love that—"the outer fringes of His works." The Contemporary English Version says it like this: "These things are merely a whisper of God's power at work. How little we would understand if this whisper ever turned into thunder!"

Moving on to the music department. Does God like rock, country and western, or classical music? I doubt He really cares, but I tend to think His favorites are those that glorify Him and edify you. He loves to hear your voice and mine as we sing praises to Him. Psalm 108:1 says, "I will sing and make music with all my soul." Paul encouraged us to "speak to one another with psalms, hymns, and spiritual songs, singing and make melody in your heart to the Lord" (Ephesians 5:19).

Last but not least, physical education. God created the heavens, earth, and man and "He saw all that He had made, and behold, it was very good" (Genesis 1:31). We are created in three parts: soul, body, and spirit (1 Thessalonians 5:23). When one part is ailing, it can affect all parts. "Do you not know that your body is a temple of the Holy Spirit, who is in you, whom you have from God, and that you are not your own?" (1 Corinthians 6:19). Be nice to your body, giving focus to all areas.

Webster's Collegiate Dictionary gives this theological definition of economy: the Creator's plan; the design of Providence. In God's economy, there is a plan to carry out His perfect will in the lives of His chosen ones, and His timing is perfect. Each one spends his or her allotted time in each classroom of grace, as the Spirit of God tenderly leads every child in order that they may receive "the unfathomable riches of Christ" (Ephesians 3:8).

God desires to dispense all that He has and all that He is into His creation as the utmost expression of Himself. He is our life; He is our sustenance; He is our everything. "And my God will supply all your needs according to His riches in glory in Christ Jesus" (Philippians 4:19).

Father God, help us to be patient in Your classroom of grace. Let us not compare ourselves against another but only unto Christ. Thank you for training us up to do the work to which You have called us. Mold us; shape us after Your will and in Your timing. Our trust is in You, Lord. In Jesus's name, amen.

What's that Smell?

Have you ever walked into your house and been hit with a smell that nearly knocked you over? Perhaps you detected it by merely walking into a particular area of a room. One thing is for sure—when that happens, we become Sherlock Holmes with our noses.

After waking one morning, I shuffled into my kitchen with one eye open on the way to make my ritualistic pot of coffee. Midway across the kitchen, my sensory awareness reached red level proportions. I detected that single, distinctive odor that comes only from something either very rotten or very dead.

I opened my refrigerator to see if the offender might be hiding there and decided it was not. I sniffed the kitchen sink for looming leftovers lurking in the disposal. It was clear. I then opened the pantry, where my canned goods were stored.

On the floor of the pantry was a new bag of potatoes I had purchased that week. I noticed the smell intensified as I closed in on that particular area. I picked up the bag to find a disgusting, mushy, stomach-turning potato in the very bottom of the bag. I had located my smelly culprit.

As it turned out, it was not going to be as simple as just getting rid of the odious tuber. The foulness had actually leaked through a ventilation hole in the bag and into the carpet, leaving its rancid residue. I tried cleaning it first with a soapy solution, but the smell remained. I tried ammonia solutions; it still came back. It took several tries with different solutions before finally removing the stench permanently.

It reminds me of how sin can creep into our lives unsuspectingly. It can hide behind perfectly normal everyday activities. Then one day it reveals itself in most unpleasant ways.

The consequences of sin are always an unwanted and unwelcome perpetrator. Like the rotten smell of the decomposing potato, the stench of sin can sink in deeply, buried behind pride, selfishness, and rebellion. Its rancid repercussions can last for many years, even into future generations (Numbers 14:18). It is the nature of the beast.

As Christians, we are to deal with sin immediately. To allow it to remain gives opportunity for sin to worsen into a much larger and deeper transgression. The problem arises when we ignore sinful behavior or attempt to wash it off with "We're only human." Many Christians settle for that excuse. But God has called us to a life of purity and holiness, not a life of defending our carnality.

The good news as Christians is that our sins are forgiven. First John 1:9 says, "If we confess our sins, He is faithful and just to forgive us our sins and to cleanse us from all unrighteousness." As we confess our sins, when God looks at us, He sees the blood of Christ and not our sin. Refusal to confess is selfish pride.

Second Timothy 2:19 declares, "Nevertheless, the firm foundation of God stands, bearing this seal, 'The Lord knows those who are His,' and, 'everyone who names the name of the Lord is to abstain from sin.'"

Almighty God, we cast down every high thing that exalts itself against the knowledge of God and bring every sinful thought captive unto the obedience of Christ. We thank You that when we confess our sins, You are faithful to forgive us and to cleanse us from all unrighteousness. Our daily individual prayer, Father, is, "If I call You my Savior, may my life reflect that You are also my Lord."

I Surrender All

"All to Jesus I surrender; all to Him I freely give…"

I have sung that song numerous times throughout the years, hearing it first in a tiny congregation as a small child. It is among my list of favorite old hymns. Sadly, for years, I only regurgitated the words without really hearing them.

Years ago, I sat with an individual, both discussing how we always desired to give 100 percent in anything we set our minds or our hands to. We boasted about our perfectionism, as if it defined our very character. After all, Albert Einstein said, "Weakness of attitude becomes weakness of character."

A few days later, on a Sunday evening, I lay in bed unable to sleep. The message that morning in church had spoken to me, and I wrestled with my faith in that moment. After several minutes, I brazenly beckoned Almighty God.

"Lord," I said, "what is wrong? Something is missing!" I then began, one by one, to recite my religious resume of the past several years to Him (as if He needed that). At that very moment, God answered in two ingenious ways.

First, He immediately brought to mind the conversation I had earlier in the week of my self-congratulatory perfectionism. Then He added, in what seemed an audible voice, "You've given all of yourself to everything but Me." He said, "I need *all* of you."

My heart sank, and I knew He was right. In that moment, at the foot of the cross, in the presence of a holy God, I repented of my selfish pride and surrendered my life to God—100 percent. God immediately blessed it with a tremendous hunger and thirst for Him and His Word.

Surrender tends to drum up negative connotations, as if surrender naturally means someone loses. Some may even want to portray God as some sort of burglar holding us at gunpoint, forcing us to give Him everything. However, when we come to know and understand the true nature of God, we discover how false that image is.

Mark recorded the words of Jesus in 8:34–36: "If anyone wishes to come after Me, let him deny himself, and take up his cross and follow Me. For whoever wishes to save his life shall lose it; but whoever loses his life for My sake…shall save it. For what does it profit a man to gain the whole world, and lose his soul?"

In chapter 10, Mark records how the rich young ruler fell to his knees asking Jesus how he could inherit the eternal life of which Jesus had spoken.

Moments later, he boasted of his self-righteousness as he struggled between Law and Grace. Jesus, knowing the rich man's heart, replied, "One thing you lack: go and sell all you possess, and give to the poor, and you shall have treasure in heaven; and come, follow Me" (Mark 10:21). However, the man's face fell at the words of Jesus, and he went away grieving. (Mark 10: 22) So close … and yet so far.

Was God telling me to stop giving 100 percent of myself in my work? Absolutely not. I believe God's people should be some of the *best* in productivity. What He *was* telling me was simply to keep Him *first,* to let go of my prideful performance and offer my work as a reflection of God's treasure hidden in my heart.

In my early years I was immature in my understanding, believing that salvation was supposed to automatically make me "think and behave" differently. Imagine my confusion when it did not. What was required was dying to self—surrendering, which then enabled me to worship and truly enjoy God on a daily basis.

Surrendering to God frees us from those things we hold on to that essentially hold us back from God's best for our lives. Surrendering brings us to the place where we find ourselves *wanting* to put God first. Surrender is a *choice,* and it is a choice that we make every moment of every day in every situation and circumstance, enabling us to follow Christ with our whole heart.

Father, we pray for those who are struggling in their faith, wondering why they feel something is missing. We pray that Your grace would envelop their heart, soul, and mind, bringing them to the place of sweet surrender. Bless them, Father, with a hunger and thirst for Your Word. And for those who know not of Your salvation, we pray that their hearts be softened toward you. Bless them with holy companions of encouragement. In Jesus's name, amen.

"But Who Do You Say I Am?"

I love the story from the book of Matthew when Jesus and his disciples arrive in a particularly pagan area. Jesus asked his followers, "Who do people say that the Son of Man is?" (Matthew 16:13).

The disciples answered with a variety of names derived from a mixture of ideologies. "Some say John the Baptist; others, Elijah; but still others, Jeremiah, or one of the prophets" (Matthew 16:14).

Then Jesus turned to His disciples and asked a simple yet most profound question: "But who do you say that I am?" (Matthew 16:15)

Most everyone has a favorite scripture. This is one that I call my "signature scripture." Several years ago, I found myself in a place of searching. I had known and revered the Lord since I was a small child, but as an adult I had grown complacent in my faith walk. Frankly, I had become quite stagnant, but God had already begun a work in me, beckoning me to draw closer. I prayed and asked that God would create a hunger in my spirit, not only for His Word, but also for the things of God.

I dusted off a Bible I had received as a gift years earlier and developed a plan. I was going to start with the New Testament, beginning with Matthew. I was already familiar with many of the stories, but I noticed as I continued to read that something else was happening. As if a veil was lifting from my eyes, my understanding of what I was reading was changing, and halfway through the sixteenth chapter of Matthew, a light came on!

"But who do you say that I am?" The words nearly leapt from the page. I could not go any further. I hung on those eight tiny words.

"But who do *you* say that I am?" I sensed the Lord was asking me directly the one truly revealing question of where I was in my walk with the Him. Confronted by the shallowness of my own life, I contemplated the depth of that simple yet profound question.

Who did my language say that He was? Who did my thoughts say that He was? Who did my actions say that Jesus was? Everything I said or did, I realized, was a reflection of who Jesus was in my life. I had been guilty of putting Him in a box, pulling Him out on Sundays, and using Him only in the case of emergencies. My heart was heavy from the weight of my superficial faith.

However, joy and restoration came as I read the next two verses. Simon Peter replied, "You are the Christ, the Son of the Living God" (Matthew 16:16).

Jesus answered, saying, "Blessed are you, Simon, for flesh and blood have not revealed this to you, but My Father who is in heaven" (Matthew 16:17).

In that moment I knew beyond any doubt that, just like Simon Peter, God was revealing himself to me in a way that would affect me forever. That tiny, simple scripture held a mirror to my soul and became the springboard of my faith.

Jesus knew the heart of Simon Peter; He wanted Peter to know too. The same is true for each of us. But who do *you* say that He is?

Your Word, O Lord, lifts the veil from our eyes and reveals the mystery of Christ to those who hunger and thirst for righteousness. Forgive us, Father, for the complacency in our lives that has blurred our walk with You. Thank you for restoring our spiritual vision that we might see the kingdom of God. Reveal to us those things that have kept us from living a life that truly reflects the character of Christ. Empower us by the Holy Spirit to be bold witnesses for You. In Jesus's name, amen.

Heaven's Dress Code

In the summer of 1984, my husband and I vacationed at a fancy resort well above our economic level. One evening, our boredom and impulsivity led us from our hotel to a very ritzy dinner club whose entrance resembled the massive, heavily carved wooden doors of a castle. Upon entering, the bold and brassy "big band" sound confirmed we were definitely out of our league.

A well-dressed gentleman with a genteel flair and a semi-British brogue hastily greeted us and asked if we had reservations; we did not. Giving my husband a rather haughty "once over", he graciously informed us that we were still *able* to dine with them, and then inquired of our familiarity with the restaurant's dress code.

The look on his face, as well as ours, was a dead giveaway to our ignorance of the pompous policy. Obviously, crisp blue jeans and the new Izod pullover fell short of the restaurant's standards. Fortunately, the dinner club was equipped for the "etiquettely challenged" and quickly whisked my husband off to a well-furnished coatroom. Soon he returned, donned with the most hideous sky blue and gold plaid jacket resembling a poorly dressed used car salesman.

Religious perceptions can often lead us to have similar ideas about our spiritual attire. Man often conceives a variety of methods in which he believes he can obtain entrance into the kingdom of heaven. Many try putting on goodness, power, self-righteousness, and even living by the Ten Commandments (or some of them anyway), however, *all fall short of God's standards.*

Isaiah 61:10 says, "For He has clothed me with garments of salvation; He has wrapped me with a robe of righteousness."

The kingdom of God requires a dress code—the garment of salvation—and Jesus Christ stands at the door of our hearts to dine with all who receive Him. "Yet to all who received him, to those who believed in his name, he gave the right to become children of God" (John 1:12).

Matthew recorded Jesus's words regarding the only way into the kingdom. Jesus said, "Not everyone who says to Me, 'Lord, Lord,' will enter the kingdom of heaven; but he who does the will of My Father who is in heaven" (Matt. 7:21).

He went on to say many would argue with Him, delivering a lengthy congratulatory recital of their religious resumes. Jesus added, "And then I will declare to them, 'I never knew you; depart from Me, you who practice lawlessness'" (Matt. 7:22–23).

The shed blood of Jesus Christ clothes us with salvation, giving us atonement or a "covering" for our sinful flesh, making us holy and acceptable in His sight. While it is a covering, completely satisfying Almighty God, we still find that we struggle with our sin nature, the flesh.

To be "wrapped in the robe of righteousness" is to "put on Christ." We do this not just on Sundays only, but every day, that others will see the righteousness of Christ in us and through us. We are, after all, representatives of the King!

Brother or sister in Christ, righteousness is ours upon receiving Him as Savior, but we must take hold of what is ours and practice wearing it, making us more like Christ, being "transformed into the same image from glory to glory" (2 Corinthians 3:18). The garment of salvation saves you; the robe of righteousness sets you apart. Did you put on Christ today?

Holy God, we thank You for the gift of Jesus Christ. May we be found in Him, not having a righteousness of our own derived from the law, but the righteousness that comes from God on the basis of faith. We greatly rejoice that upon receiving Christ as Savior, we are clothed with garments of salvation and given a robe of righteousness. Help us to be sensitive to the leading of the Holy Spirit as we work out our salvation with awe and reverence, daily putting on the righteousness of Christ. In Jesus's name, amen.

Precious Testimonies

Teaching Bible stories to kindergartners is both challenging and rewarding. My husband's description of working with little ones is, "like lining up grasshoppers," and I think it fits perfectly for that age group. As a Vacation Bible School volunteer, I had signed up to teach this lively class.

Having memorized the stories in order to retell them effectively, I sat on the floor amid the young grasshoppers. As I spoke, one little girl began to wriggle her way toward the front, settling directly in front of me. She was listening intently to the story of Joseph and his coat of many colors. Her eyes were locked and intense as she began to lean forward with curiosity.

Recognizing that I was wooing her with my enlivened message, I looked directly at her as I spoke, and she nudged in even closer. With wide eyes, she gingerly raised her hand. I paused to allow her innocent query.

"Do you have on lipstick?" she questioned in a loud whisper.

My bubble burst as I realized I had "captured" her, not by my energetic reiteration of the story of Joseph's coat, but rather the shiny pink coat on my lips.

Sharing God's Word with others is both challenging and rewarding. If you've ever sat across from junior high or high school students and watched as their eyes glaze over, you know what I'm talking about.

But the key is *just do it!* Share the good news of Jesus Christ! It doesn't matter if you haven't memorized all the scripture you promised you would. If you know Jesus Christ, He is all you need!

When Jesus called Saul (who we know as Paul), he had not spent years in seminary. In fact, he had been actively persecuting Christians. What could Jesus possibly see in him, and what did he have that he could possibly share with others?

When Paul arrived in Damascus following his conversion, and after Ananias restored his sight, "he immediately began to proclaim Jesus saying, 'He is the Son of God'" (Acts 9:20). All Paul had was a genuine encounter with Christ. He had a life-changing experience, recognizing the depth of his sin and the wretchedness of his soul, compelling him all the more to share his experience of God's mercy and grace.

Later, when speaking to the Corinthians, Paul said,

> When I came to you, I did not come with superiority of speech or of wisdom, proclaiming to you the testimony of God. For I determined to know nothing among you except Jesus Christ, and Him crucified...My message was not in persuasive words of wisdom, but in demonstration of the Spirit and of power, that your faith should not rest on the wisdom of men, but on the power of God
>
> 1 Corinthians 2:1–5

Though the bells and whistles (and pink lipstick) may draw the crowd in, the Spirit of God alone draws the heart. Bells and whistles are only added attractions, but they are not life changing; nor will they provide you with a testimony. They are simply tools used to present the message of Christ.

You may not have had a Road to Damascus experience as Paul did. Some testimonies are certainly more *colorful* than others are, but that doesn't make your story any less valuable or effective. If you have had a personal encounter with Christ, then you have a testimony.

It is what God has delivered us from, brought us to, and led us through that become our message. It makes your story and mine real and effective to the glory and praise of God.

God of wonders, how grateful we are for the anointed ones You send to minister the message of Christ. We thank you for the work of the Holy Spirit, who draws us in at our appointed time and who will give us utterance as we faithfully give testimony to the power of God at work in our lives. All praise and glory to God our Savior!

Just As I Am

The beauty of teaching young children is the opportunity for deeper lessons springing up from the pure, unrestricted innocence and enthusiasm of youth. It was Vacation Bible School week again, and I had prepared the lesson of Jesus washing the disciples' feet for the first and second grade classes.

Prior to the lesson, I was trying to figure out a way to *dirty* the feet of a few of the children. Originally, I decided I would elect two or three children to remove their shoes, go outside, and grind their feet into the dirt and grass; but that morning, it had begun to rain, and I knew that would prove disastrous. I decided we would simply pretend.

As the children began to assemble, I noticed one small boy, dirty, unkempt, and wearing mismatched and tattered clothes. His bare feet looked as though he had walked through black soot. All the other children were wearing shoes. Knowing the innocence of children can sometimes be brutally honest, I was concerned that someone might call attention to his feet. I wondered how I would approach this without embarrassing the boy, so I quietly prayed for a new plan.

Hoping that no one else had already noticed his feet, I instructed the children to form a circle on the floor, sitting on their knees. In the center of the circle, I placed a large bowl of water. As I neared the feet washing part of the story, I told of how dirty the disciples' feet became in Jesus' day, as most wore sandals or even walked barefoot.

I said, "I planned to go outside and get our feet really dirty. However, today it's too wet, but I sure wish I had someone with dirty feet like the disciples might have had."

As if on cue, the boy's hand shot up as he shouted, "Oh, look, teacher! I do. See? Use my feet!" He willingly, shamelessly, and joyfully offered himself and his feet, *just as he was,* to the assistance of the lesson. He was my hero that day.

The feet washing ceremony, as John recorded in 13:1–12, reveals more than just the act of cleansing. It is a lesson in humility for both parties involved. It is just as much a service to our Lord to offer ourselves humbly, just as we are, as to lovingly wash the feet of another.

"Then He poured the water into the basin and began to wash the disciples' feet and to wipe them with a towel." At first, Simon Peter refused to have his feet washed by Jesus. Jesus responded by saying, "What I do, you do not realize now, but you shall understand later" (John 13:5–7).

Jesus continued, saying, "He who has already bathed needs only to wash his feet, but is completely clean" (John 13:10).

Upon repentance, baptism, and receiving God's Holy Spirit, we are, in God's eyes, perfectly clean. However, our human nature is still very much a part of us and is in need of frequent cleansing.

First John 1:9 reminds us that "if we confess our sins, He is faithful and just to forgive us our sins and to cleanse us from all unrighteousness."

Confession is imperative if our walk is to be holy and upright. Unconfessed sin in the Christian hinders our close relationship with Christ, preventing us from walking in complete victory. Recognizing our sin and allowing God to cleanse us once again restores the confidence in our walk with Him. Confess often, keeping short accounts with God.

The young boy that day allowed more than just a timely prop for our lesson. He demonstrated a greater example in the act of cleansing. He openly acknowledged his uncleanness and offered himself joyfully, allowing the teacher to wash his soiled feet. May we allow God to use us, offering ourselves to Him . . . just as we are.

Father, we pray that we might have a servant's heart to symbolically wash the feet of another through mercy and grace. Convict our hearts of any unconfessed sin that we may turn it over to You, for the sacrifices You recognize are a broken and repentant heart. Wash us thoroughly from our iniquities, and cleanse us in the precious blood of the righteous and holy Lamb of God. In Jesus's name we pray, amen.

It Must Be the Glasses

Years ago, I resigned myself to the fact that it was wiser for me to spend less on cheap sunglasses than to suffer the costly loss of an expensive pair. I have left them in restaurants, bathrooms, and shoe departments as well as the fruit section of the grocery store.

I have indeed spent a sufficient amount of time spinning the display column of sunglasses, trying on pair after pair in search of suitable sunshades. For years, I determined I had the worst luck finding a pair that was not crooked. I eventually accepted the crooked shades as one of the drawbacks of buying cheap glasses and continued until I found a pair I liked. I would purchase them and immediately begin reshaping what the manufacturer never could seem to get right.

Then one day, I had a "eureka moment" while

sitting across from my eye doctor as he fit me with a new pair of eyeglasses. He placed the glasses on me, wiggled them a bit, pulled them off, and then tried again. With a slight grin he finally stated, "Hmmm. Your ears are a little crooked."

What? No way. Give me a mirror. How dare he tell me my ears are crooked! It's gotta be the glasses!

Now, as my doctor, I knew he was there for my good—to make sure my vision and comfort were the best they could be. That meant my glasses needed to fit properly. It was not a big deal, just a simple adjustment of one of the earpieces...*just as I had always done with my cheap sunglasses*. It was then I realized I had been angry all those years with the manufacturers of the sunglasses for unfounded reasons. The problem was with *me*, not the sunglasses!

We all occasionally find ourselves in a position of receiving corrective instruction. I would venture to say our initial knee-jerk reaction is, "What? No way! What gives you the right?" In a sense, we are saying, "How dare you. The problem can't be with me!"

Often, we compare ourselves against a crooked world and think we are doing pretty well. We tend to want to blame someone or something else for our circumstances, even blaming it on just plain bad luck. We put off accepting that the possible reason for chaos or conflict in our careers, family, and relationships might just be a deformed perception causing distorted choices.

To the Romans, Paul encouraged, "Do not be conformed to this world, but be transformed by the renewing of your mind, that you may prove what the will of God is, that's which is good and acceptable and perfect" (Romans 12:2).

To the Philippians, he pled, "Whatever is true, whatever is honorable, whatever is right, whatever is pure, whatever is lovely, whatever is of good repute, if there is any excellence and if anything worthy of praise, let your mind dwell on these things … and the God of peace shall be with you" (Phil. 4:8–9).

God's will for us is to live a life pleasing unto Him as well as receiving personal delight and enjoyment. We are especially blessed to enjoy a life that is honoring to God. Whether we need to tweak an attitude, a behavior, a habit, or even more extreme measures, it is not because we are so bad; it is because *God is so good.*

Father, You beckon us from Calvary's cross. Only in Christ do we find our truest measure of grace and mercy, as well as the true and holy standard by which to live. Thank you for the transforming power of Your Holy Spirit in our lives, renewing our minds that we may live a life holy and acceptable and pleasing in Your sight. Thank you for qualifying us to share in all that belongs to Your people. In Jesus's name, amen.

Keys of Wealth

God works in mysterious ways, using the most innocent, innocuous objects to remind us of His love, His providence, and His ever-present goodness. On this particular day, it all began for me in the kitchen. Here I would discover precious keys of wealth that I had tucked away and forgotten. What are the keys of wealth, you ask? The story will show you. Perhaps you too have your own keys tucked away somewhere.

They are nestled securely in nearly every kitchen junk drawer. Their unique size, shape, and finish leave us guessing what their original employment was. Once useful, they are now members of the jobless, homeless, heavy metal, "groovy" band of brothers—loose keys.

Rifling through my junk drawer—and that is what we all do unless we are June Cleaver or Martha Stewart—I came across the neglected assembly. Were they the lost souls of the key society, the penniless drifters, the down and outers? What about the shiny one that appears to be a newcomer? What's its story? Was it recently laid off?

Further study revealed much more than their disadvantaged service; it brought back a rush of memories. One key belonged to the back door of the home we had moved from several years ago. Another was our daughter's spare key to her car; actually, one of several, as it was a common practice to lose her keys. A silver key marked with pink nail polish reminded me it belonged to my sister's apartment, but she no longer lives there. I'm not sure why I have kept it.

Then I uncovered one of those odd-shaped keys, very tiny and delicate, the kind you know fits neither a car nor a door. This key belonged to a small wooden box that resembled a treasure chest. I had received it as a gift several years ago and it was now home to several personal and family valuables, but I had never locked it. Rarely opened, the chest had become simply a decorative item on a cabinet, moving it only for the occasional dusting.

That day however, finding this particular key prompted me to reopen our box of treasures. Going through it took me on the most wonderful journey, without ever leaving my living room.

The first was a palm-sized New Testament given to my husband by his great-grandmother when he was only ten. Behind it was a 1926 language primer issued to my would-be-father-in-law in 1934 from a tiny, one-room country school.

Tears filled my eyes as I held the copy of the first letter I had written to the family of my transplant donor. It holds a place of honor among my treasures, along with the page torn from a calendar the day of my surgery. Beside it was a handwritten letter from our comedic son during his first year of college. As I read it, I broke out into laughter.

Pictures, cards, napkins, brochures, and my grandparents' tattered and dog-eared Bible replayed years of memories, sparking laughter, tears, thankfulness, and wonderment. Near the bottom, I found precious tokens of bereavement from loved ones I miss dearly, sharply snapping my mind back into the living room.

My journey that day began in a junk drawer as I took a brief walk down the memory lane of old used keys. Finding the tiniest of keys, however, would lead me to revisit a few of my life's treasured memories buried deeply in a forgotten chest. A brief exploration through my special wooden box would reveal precious memories of my family and friends, as well as the immense generosity of the human spirit. Most of all, it revealed the ever-present hand of God always at work in my life. Yes, God works in mysterious ways!

Father, I thank You for the little reminders that You lovingly and ingeniously place into our hectic lives that work to freshen our spirit, stir our soul, and bring a smile to our face. I pray we be ever attentive to Your leading, that we might recognize those tender God moments and praise You in and for them. You are the ever-loving and everlasting Father.

Land of the Living

One day each year, we celebrate the twenty-four hours that literally saved my life. On August 8, 2001, I received the precious gift of an organ transplant. In transplant groups, they call me a "survivor" according to the number of years, but I prefer to say, like everyone else who takes a breath every morning, "It's great to be alive." No life expectancy frames, but also no grandiose expectations of immortality either. As they say, "One day at a time."

As I opened my Bible one morning, I noticed several scriptures I had penned on the back inside pages. Some had dates, leaving me wondering why I had noted it at that particular time. Other scriptures had comments in parentheses reminding me of their distinction. Two, however, earned a position of merit in the upper corner rather than the random placement of the others.

Psalm 118:17 and Psalm 27:13 are scriptures of the realization of looming death while holding on to the hope of life, placing our trust and confidence in the will and work of God.

Psalm 118:17 says, "I shall not die, but live, and tell of the works of the Lord." Originally, I had noted and claimed this for our cancer-stricken pastor in 1994. I gained strength in observing how his sermons grew more powerful as his body grew weaker.

Little did I know I would be claiming it yet again a few years later when, in 1997, I was diagnosed with a disease giving me less than five years to live. Blood drawn during a routine physical eventually led the doctors to the discovery of an autoimmune disorder that had been silently destroying my liver, as well as other smaller organs, for years. We would learn later that the five-year life expectancy would only be four.

In February of 2001, I awoke from a dream with the most ominous presence around me. In the dream I heard a voice shrouded by darkness speak the date of August 19. Puzzled, I wanted to believe it to be my coming transplant date, but I could not shake the feeling of darkness and gloom that had so engulfed me. So I rose and returned to the Scriptures.

I turned to Psalm 27, a psalm of David of trusting in the Lord without fear. The psalm begins with "The Lord is my light and my salvation, whom shall I fear?" I continued to read, trying to shake the menacing feeling. Then my eyes fell upon verses 13 and 14, and I wept.

"I would have despaired unless I had believed I would see the goodness of the Lord in the land of the living. Wait for the Lord; be strong and let your heart take courage; yes, wait for the Lord."

"Yes!" I shouted to the darkness. "Did you hear that? It says, 'In the land of the living!'"

My eternal soul was secure, but I wanted to believe the Lord for the here and now, in *this* life—the land of the *living!* Though not my will, but His, I knew He was moving me into a place where He would show me that indeed I needed to "be still, and know that He was God" while learning to trust Him with my life—literally.

The ominous feeling, however, did not leave. Perhaps it is a feeling only those who are gravely ill can understand. Nevertheless, August was rapidly approaching, and I was getting weaker. Though I attempted to hide it from family and friends, I knew I could not survive to see my October birthday.

Then the call came late evening on August 7, 2001. After hours of preparation, followed by seven hours in transplant surgery, the doctor finally consulted with my anxious family. My surgeon spoke in amazement at how it appeared that tiny veins were miraculously melding together during the reconstruction. Then he informed them of the news I would learn a while later—that I would not have survived even two more weeks without the transplant. What would have been the month of my funeral became the month of celebration!

So, was August 19 to be the date of my death or perhaps my funeral? I will never know this side of heaven. I do know that the thief, the prince of darkness, "comes to kill, steal, and destroy; but Jesus came that I may have life, and might have it abundantly" (John 10:10). For now, though, August 19 no longer matters. What mattered in those crucial moments was that my faith and my hope rested in the word of God.

Death was defeated that day as we beheld the "goodness of the Lord in the land of the living" through His perfect timing and His hand in the surgery, as well as in the many days and months that followed. I have never ceased to stand amazed at the mighty works of our heavenly Father.

Whatever struggle, illness, or loss you may be going through, I encourage you to turn to the word of God for your strength, your peace, and your comfort. Allow the Lord to wash over your fears, your darkness, and your pain with the water of His Word. May your heart take courage today; be strong and wait for the Lord. For through we may not always understand, His timing is always perfect.

We thank you, Father, that in our darkest hours, we find our strength, our peace, and our comfort in Your Word. Though we may never fully understand, we know that Your ways and Your timing is always perfect, and we will spend the rest of our days telling of Your goodness in the land of the living! All glory, power, and honor are Yours, Almighty God and Eternal Lord. Hallelujah to our King!

No Stuff, Just Fluff

Twinkies were declared "the snack of the Depression" during the 1930s. In addition, because of their nearly endless (and scary) shelf life, they were a staple in the 1960s bomb shelters. But for me, they are and forever will be on my "Thou Shalt Not Eat" list.

It has nothing to do with any religious practice, resolution, or even dietary restrictions. Simply put, they are among the top ten on my "Gwish Factor" list. What is the Gwish Factor, you ask?

It is any jelly, pudding, or saucy surprise hidden inside unsuspecting food. Included on the list are Ding Dongs, calzones, cream-filled cakes, and the bursting-at-the-seams jelly-filled doughnut, which registers about a 9.5 on the Gwish Factor Scale. I love surprises, just not in my food!

I like my food straight up, with no funny stuff and no fluff. Though I would never be considered a health food nut, I do like to keep things as close to nature as possible. Moreover, there is not one single natural thing about a Twinkie! They rank even less in nutritional value. Sorry, Twinkies!

Just as we should be prudent about the nutritional value of the food we consume, so should we be discerning about our spiritual nutrition. It seems as if the delivery of the gospel at times has become as fluffy as our snack foods. Over the years, some teachers and preachers have yielded to "feel good" messages to appease the crowd, and members who rely solely upon their message walk around filled with emotional fluff but no spiritual sustenance.

Heresy had entered into the church at Colossae. Paul, an apostle of Jesus Christ, had a deep concern for the Colossians to come to a deeper understanding of the person and power of Christ. Paul knew that a proper view of Christ was the perfect antidote for heresy. Devotion and obedience to the true gospel would strengthen their walk and help them to resist opposing attitudes and influences.

One of my favorite prayers from God's Word is that of Paul for the Colossians in the first chapter, verses 9–14. Paul was thanking them for their faithfulness and for the love they showed for each other. He then shared a page from his prayer journal, saying,

> For this reason ... we have not ceased to pray for you and to ask that you may be filled with the knowledge of His will in all spiritual wisdom and understanding, so that you may walk in a manner worthy of the Lord, to please Him in all respects, bearing fruit in every good work and increasing in the knowledge of God.
>
> Colossians 9–10

To know and understand God's will for our lives in true godly wisdom and understanding empowers us to do so much more than just get a temporary filling on a Sunday morning. It gives us a continuous fulfillment that pleases God and bears the fruit of righteousness with a hunger to know God even more.

To fill ourselves with fluffy, feel-good emotions may make us feel better for a moment, but it is crippling to our spiritual walk. Moreover, it renders us malnourished and fruitless, as well as helpless, when confronted by opposing influences. We are oozing in sweetness but lacking in spiritual power! Fluff belongs only in our food, but ... I still think I will pass.

God of wonders! To know You fully is to love You completely. You are before all things, and in You all things hold together. Thank you, Father, that You have qualified us to share in the inheritance of the holy ones. Fill us with the knowledge of Your will that we may bear good fruit, pleasing You in all respects. In Jesus's name, amen.

This Is a Test

Though I haven't noticed them in a long time, as a child it seemed television networks ran system checks quite often. When they did, a very official-sounding voice interrupted the programming with, "This is a test of the Emergency Broadcast System. For the next sixty seconds, this station will conduct a test ... The broadcasters of your area ... have developed this system to keep you informed in the event of an emergency. This is only a test."

Then, for the next thirty seconds or so, a long, eerie, high-pitched, monotone sound filled the room as a brightly colored EBS logo mesmerized you into a nearly hypnotic state. The test finally ended with the comforting words, "If this had been an actual emergency, you would have been instructed where to tune in your area for news and official information."

Because I was young and still possessed fears of the boogieman, the test sent shivers down my spine. *What emergency?* I wondered. I had disturbing visuals of "the Russians charging through my back door." Silly I know; however, during the sixties, that notion was very real.

Life brings intermittent tests—usually when you least expect it. We tend to think of testing only in the bigger things, like an illness or job loss. Tests, however, appear almost daily—like the fender bender in your new car, the overdraft notice, or the not-so-positive note from the school principal regarding your child.

Each instance is secretly testing our personal emergency systems, each one quietly teaching us something about ourselves. Many tests last no more than thirty or sixty seconds and then are over; others last much longer and test you much deeper.

Years ago, as a young and fiery new Christian, I was determined to "go where no man had gone before." The Holy Spirit lit a fire in me that consumed me day and night. One day, I prayed Psalm 26:2 to God: "Examine me, O Lord, and try me; Test my mind and my heart." I had spent five years in an in-depth and thorough study of His Word. Naïve and brazen, I wanted to be tested.

Not long afterward, I discovered I was gravely ill, and I remember thinking, *This isn't exactly what I had in mind*. Nevertheless, it was mine, and at times it seemed the tortuous monotone sound of fear and dread attempted to mesmerize me into a state of panic and depression.

God was so precious, however, to prepare me years before for what I was completely unaware of, and now it was time to put what I knew to a bigger test. It was the moment of "an actual emergency," and because I had spent years in the Word, I knew just where to go to for "news and official information."

Jesus said, "Come unto Me, all who are weary and heavy-laden, and I will give you rest. Take my yoke upon you and learn from Me, for I am gentle and humble in heart; and you shall find rest for your souls" (Matthew 11:28).

How often do we find ourselves complaining about things that really are not that important? We neglect to recognize that everything is in preparation for what lies ahead. Our blessed Lord gives us minor interruptions in order to assure us of our preparedness for real emergencies.

Jesus reminds us of what lies ahead with these words: "I have told you these things, so that in Me you may have peace. In this world, you will have trouble, but take heart! I have overcome the world" (John 16:33 NIV).

Lord, I thank you that we are invited to come to You when we are weary and laden with the burdens that weigh us down. Help us, Father, by Your spirit, to heed the minor things and learn from them in order to prepare us for our actual emergencies. Let us be mindful that You are our ever present help in time of trouble. You are our overcomer! In Jesus's name, amen.

Inquiring Minds

My family calls me the Google guru. I suppose I am guilty as charged, as I am an information junkie. I have never been satisfied *that* something is the way it is; I have always wanted to know *why* something is the way it is. Thus I spend a good deal of time in books or on the Internet searching and researching facts, theories, commentaries, and whatever else brings a question to my mind. Just for fun, I also enjoy exploring useless bits of information, also known as UBIs.

Recently, I was on my way home from a neighboring city, slurping down my favorite cherry-lime slush. Within seconds, I was experiencing the phenomenon we have all endured at some time in our lives—the ever-dreaded brain freeze! So I decided to add "brain freeze" to my personal UBI list.

A quick online search found the scientific name of brain freeze is *sphenopalatine gangleoneuralgia*. Exactly! Brain freeze is much easier. It occurs from our body's reaction to the extreme cold hitting the palate. The blood flow immediately shuts down in that area in an attempt to minimize loss of body heat. The fluctuation in vessel constriction then causes the pain we know as brain freeze. A quick drink of warm or room-temperature liquid or even rubbing the tongue against the roof of the mouth will bring things back to normal. So, now you know!

The Lord said in Hosea 4:6, "My people are destroyed for lack of knowledge." Proverbs, the book of wisdom, says, "There is gold, and an abundance of jewels; But the lips of knowledge are a more precious thing" (Proverbs 20:15 MSG).

Though I doubt our knowledge of the science behind the brain freeze will win us any awards, it is the discipline of study itself that opens doors to new discoveries or perhaps personal eureka moments. Many times, it is a deeper understanding of the simplest things that can actually improve our daily lives.

God's Word from the New Testament, however, goes on to issue a warning about the gathering of much knowledge. Second Timothy 3:7 speaks of those who are "always learning and never able to come to the knowledge of the truth." Additionally, Ecclesiastes 1:18 reminds us of the great burden that accompanies the gathering of much knowledge.

It is the desire of God, our Savior, for all men to be saved and to come to the knowledge of the truth. John recorded Jesus's words in John 8:32: "And you shall know the truth and the truth shall make you free."

It is important for us to realize, however, that individually, truth alone does not set us free but rather it is the *knowledge* of the truth. Each must obtain the knowledge of this truth for his or herself. Jesus is the way, the truth, and the life, and no one comes to the Father through the knowledge of anything else but Christ.

Do you know the truth? Do you know Christ Jesus?

Father, we thank you for speaking to us through Your Word and for teaching us through life's circumstances. In our quest for knowledge, give us discernment, that we might not be deceived. Pour out Your spirit, causing us to hunger for truth, coming to a saving knowledge of Christ Jesus. Let our constant prayer be that we might know the truth that sets us free! Amen.

Are You for Real?

In the 1960s, a popular game show aired called "To Tell the Truth." The show consisted of three contestants and four celebrity judges. The contestants walked out on stage and stood before the judges and audience, all claiming to be the same person. Of course, the object of the game was for the judges to pose questions, along with clever quips, in order to determine the real person named.

Panel judges had only minutes to decide who was authentic and who the imposters were. The judges reached their final decision not only from the contestant's answers but also from carefully observing their body language. Following the individual assessment and conclusion of the judges, the game host then presented the central question of the show: "Will the real (John Doe) please stand up?" Oh, how I miss those old game shows!

We have a similar challenge as Christians to prove the validity of our faith in a perplexing and scrutinizing world. Sadly, many professing believers do not appear to be much different in behavior from unbelievers, speaking the same vulgar language, passing on the same dirty jokes, and engaging in the same ungodly behaviors as before conversion. It is no wonder Christians are not taken more seriously.

I will never forget one of my "ah-ha" moments several years ago while working part time in a public office alongside our pastor's wife. She and I walked into a crowd of people, and someone remarked, "Oh boy! Now we have to watch our language. The pastor's wife is here." Of course, we all graciously laughed, but I walked away thinking, *And what am I? Chopped liver?*

What the moment revealed is that the world *does* recognize righteousness and *is* affected by it, even if only temporarily. I also recognized the importance of the *lay-Christian* to live a life that truly reflects the light of Christ. Pastors and their wives carry a title known by the community. For the rest of us, it is less obvious. We can wear Christian T-shirts, sport "Jesus Saves" decals on our vehicles, or wear a cross around our neck, but it will be the day-to-day dealings in life that truly reveal who we are and *whose* we are.

It does not require a degree in theology to do that. Paul said, "My message and my preaching were not in persuasive words of wisdom but in demonstration of the Spirit and of power" (1 Corinthians 2:4). Paul's message was a very simple one. He preached the word of the cross and Christ crucified. It is foolishness to the lost, but it is the very power of God to those who are being saved!

Like it or not, the world is watching Christians, usually to herald claims of hypocrisy or broadcast their transgressions from the rooftops. So since we have their attention, why not use it wisely? Throw off our chameleon disguises of worldliness and stand before them in the Spirit and power available to us in Christ.

What would our words and our body language say about our identity in Christ? If the final question asked were, "Would the real followers of Jesus Christ please stand up?" would we prove to be authentic? More importantly, how do we fare before a holy God?

Lord, as we take You as Savior, may we never neglect to serve You as Lord. Forgive us for our spiritual laziness. Ignite our hearts, Lord, to stand boldly before the world, preaching salvation through Christ and Christ crucified. We pray that our actions and our words would reveal the Holy Spirit at work in us. In Jesus's name, amen.

Fit for the Kingdom

"*Oh where, oh where have my coffee cups gone? Oh where, oh where can they be?*"

I playfully sing to myself as I prepare to pour a to-go cup of coffee, trying to locate the insolated cup and companion lid. It is not that I am lacking for lids, as the ratio of lids to mugs collected over the years is nearly ten to one.

I don't know exactly the day or time of the great coffee mug exodus, but I'm pretty sure either myself or other members of my family are involved. However, one by one, they left behind a lid designed to fit one cup and one cup only. Alas, I have a drawer full of lonely mates holding on to the hope that one day its long-lost companion will return.

There have been times I thought I had the correct lid, only to experience the invigorating sensation of piping hot liquid down the front of my blouse several miles from home. Other times, I have upset a full cup of hot coffee while enthusiastically persuading the mug to accept the alien lid.

"Putting on Christ" presented a similar frustration when I came to the Lord several years ago. I had collected quite an assortment of wrong thought patterns and preconceived ideas about what I thought it meant to be a Christian. I owned a couple of Bibles, a few cassette tapes, and even fewer books that unassumingly resided on the bottom shelf behind the collection of old high school and college yearbooks and eight-track tapes.

The problem was that my old habits and ideas did not fit with the new way of life. Oh, there were times it seemed to work, only to later experience the upset or even pain of the conflicting behaviors. Forcing old habits or mindsets to fit with the will of God not only caused me to become frustrated, but I also began to doubt that my salvation had been genuine.

"Therefore if any man is in Christ, he is a new creature; the old things passed away; behold, new things have come" (2 Corinthians 5:17). My miscalculation was in assuming God would zap everything bad at the moment of salvation. Though I was a new creature in Christ, I still had a collection of old ways I was in the habit of using.

God, in His love, is patient toward us. Salvation is ours the moment we believe in our hearts and confess with our mouth that Jesus Christ is Lord. However, sanctification is a process that takes time, submission as well. The Spirit of God is at work in us. As we learn to submit more of our life to Him,

He will remove those things that do not line up with His will.

To the Romans Paul said to "put on the Lord Jesus Christ" (13:14). To the Christians in Ephesus Paul wrote, "Put on the new self, which in the likeness of God has been created in righteousness and holiness" (4:24). To the Colossians, he wrote, "Put on the new self who is being renewed to a true knowledge according to the image of the One who created him" (3:10).

Putting on Christ is to put on a renewed nature, which He fits onto us. We "put on Christ" in faith, so that He becomes ours and we become His. Trying to force fit anything else just won't work.

Father, we bow our knees unto You, acknowledging Your holiness and our rebellion, and we humbly ask Your forgiveness. We pray, Lord, that You would grant unto us strength through Your spirit working in our inner being and that we might put on the new nature, created in Your image of righteousness and holiness. In Jesus's name, amen.

Who Dressed You?

I will never forget the embarrassment I felt one Sunday morning as we settled into "our pew" preparing for worship service. I glanced down, only to discover I was wearing one navy shoe and one black shoe. It was undeniably a noticeable mismatch. Since service had already begun, it was too late to run home to change shoes. I nudged my husband and pointed out my high-heeled blunder to him, to which he replied, "So…which one of the kids dressed you this morning?"

The revelation of a personal fashion faux pas can quickly impart a lack of confidence that, if unable to correct, can accompany us throughout our entire day. The trouble zone will become our sole focus. We will find ourselves planning our entries and exits in such a way as to minimize exposure. Some may attempt a clever distraction or even create an excuse to abandon their post in search of a remedy for the fashion offense.

Why is it that it seems we are more concerned about our physical garments than we are our spiritual garments? Perhaps we either are not aware that we even *have* spiritual garments, or else we do not recognize the magnitude of their importance. Maybe we simply fail to understand that "our struggle is not against flesh and blood, but against the rulers, against darkness, against the spiritual forces of wickedness in the heavenly places" (Ephesians 6:12).

The Apostle Paul employed the knowledge he gained throughout his frequent incarcerations in structuring what is known as the "armor of God" passage. The armor and weaponry of the Roman soldier was the perfect example of what is necessary for spiritual warfare, both defensive and offensive. If anyone had an up close and personal examination of Roman armor, it was Paul.

> Finally, be strong in the Lord, and in the strength of His might. Put on the full armor of God so that you may be able to stand firm against the schemes of the devil ... Therefore, take up the full armor of God that you may be able to resist in the evil day, and having done everything, to stand firm.
>
> Ephesians 6:10–13

The scripture continues in verses 14–17, entreating us to "Stand firm then, having girded your loins with truth" (Ephesians 6:14). The belt was the first item the soldier put on and one of the most important pieces of armor, as it held everything together.

Applying the truth of God's Word at the start of each day securely fastens us with power of the word of God.

"And having put on the breastplate of righteousness..." (Ephesians 6:14). The breastplate was designed to protect the heart of the soldier. The Bible declares that the heart of man is prone to temptation (Matthew 26:41). Righteousness defends against the strategies of the devil.

"And having shod your feet with the preparation of the gospel of peace..." (Ephesians 6:15). Peace helps us to stand firmly planted on the word of God while steadying and protecting us in our daily walk through life's often-treacherous places. "He makes my feet like the feet of a deer, and makes me walk on my high places" (Habakkuk 3:19).

"In addition to all, taking up the shield of faith, by which we can extinguish all the flaming arrows of the evil one..." (Ephesians 6:16). Faith comes by hearing the word of God. Knowing the Bible and the God of the Bible gives us greater faith in trusting God as our protector.

"And take the helmet of salvation..." (Ephesians 6:17). Satan attacks the mind more than any other area, attempting to cause doubt in the assurance of our salvation. Immersing ourselves in God's Word as well as prayer brings a clear and discerning mind.

"And the sword of the Spirit, which is the word of God" (Ephesians 6:17). The sword of the spirit is the word of God. There is authority and power in the word of God. No weapon of the enemy can stand against it.

To neglect one piece of armor makes us more vulnerable to the attacks of the enemy and reduces our capacity to fully serve God. We find ourselves rationalizing our lack of preparation, making excuses, planning diversions, or perhaps even neglecting or abandoning our spiritual position altogether. Our focus will be on concealing our weakness rather than on God's call for our lives. Being "fully dressed" spiritually frees us up to *fully* do what God has called us to do.

So … who dressed you this morning?

Father, it is good for us to be dressed and equipped not only for battle, but for the peaceful days as well, for that is the time we can become most complacent. Your Word also reminds us that our battle is not against man, but against rulers and powers of darkness and against the spiritual forces of wickedness in high places revealed through the actions of man on earth. Grant us discernment in all our circumstances. We rejoice greatly as a child of God that You clothe us in the robe of righteousness, which is Christ Jesus. Great is our God and worthy of all our praise!

Out with the Bad

One day, I poured myself a glass of ice-cold orange juice. My taste buds celebrated as they anticipated the eruption of flavor flowing across my tongue. Instead, they encountered the pungent, vinegary taste of age-soured orange juice. My taste buds screamed, "Call 911!", and my body immediately responded. Fortunately, I was standing next to the kitchen sink and quickly rid myself of the rancid contents. After rinsing and gargling, I checked the date on the container to find it had gone three weeks past the sell-by date.

The physical body is quick to rid itself of anything distasteful, painful, or unpleasant. It does not need any training; it comes naturally. If we experience pain, we pull back. If unpleasant, we remove ourselves. If something tastes bad, out it comes. At least, that is if you are able to do so.

Sin is also distasteful, painful, and unpleasant. For some reason, though, it does not always provoke the same response as external stimuli do to the physical body. Additionally, the Bible acknowledges it can also be pleasurable (for a season), and that is where the problem lies. Many Christians will slip into what has been labeled as "greasy grace." "I can do what I want and then ask God for forgiveness" has been a common expression of the misunderstanding of God's grace.

The Gospel of Mark gives us a sober look at the seriousness of sin.

> If your hand causes you to sin, cut if off. It is better for you to enter eternal life maimed than with two hands to go into hell... and if your foot causes you to sin, cut it off. It is better to enter eternal life crippled than to have two feet and be thrown into hell. And if your eye causes you to sin, pluck it out.
>
> Mark 9:42–47

Now, if we take *this* particular scripture literally, we would be a congregation of maimed, crippled, and blind people. It is not exactly great recruiting material either, but Jesus was serious about getting rid of sin, and so should we.

I think a more practical interpretation today would mean to "cut off" those habits, places, maybe even people that cause or tempt us to sin. If the places your feet take you cause you to sin, cut those places off. If your eyes are causing you to think or do sinful things, cut off those subscriptions, Web sites, movies, or again, people that entice you toward sinful behavior. The same is true with the hands.

Sadly, many Christians seem to live at peace with their sin. Lust, drunkenness, greed, materialism, etc. no longer disturb us but instead seem the norm. We reason, "We're only human." Jesus did not die that we might continue to live in sin.

The antidote is *time*—time spent in prayer, in the Word, and with Jesus, the Word of Life, daily focusing and meditating on God's goodness and holiness. It is important to evaluate our actions and motives closely and continually, checking often for any distinct signs of digression. Once detected, through confession and prayer, God cleanses us from all unrighteousness.

"If we confess our sins, He is faithful and righteous to forgive us our sins and to cleanse us from all unrighteousness" (1 John 1:9).

"I acknowledged my sin to Thee, and my iniquity I did not hide" (Psalm 32:5a).

Under the leadership and direction of the Holy Spirit, the more we focus our attention on Christ, the more sin will become increasingly unpleasant and bitter. Sin eventually will become so distasteful, our immediate response will be to recoil and obediently spew it out!

Heavenly Father, You are a Holy God, and we are a sinful people. As each of us examines our own life, Lord, we are aware there is none righteous—not even one. But You have provided a way to deliver us from sin through the shed blood of Jesus Christ. Thank you that by His resurrection power we too have power and victory over sin. Hallelujah to the Lamb!

Hello, It's Me!

Today's technology allows us to make and receive phone calls as never done in past decades. Many reading this will still remember the party lines available to those living in the country where one had to wait for the neighbor to hang up in order to place a phone call. Our kids cannot imagine such barbaric forms of communication.

The nice thing about modern phone technology is you can be anywhere at any time (except for a few well-known cell phone Bermuda Triangles) and place a phone call. One can also be anywhere at any time and *receive* phone calls, many times with inopportune timing. Most public assemblies now offer as part of their standard opening the reminder for everyone to either shut off or silence all communication devices.

There have been times I have missed calls for hours because I had forgotten to reset my phone after silencing it for a meeting, leading to the frustration of friends or family members. I also have missed calls, not because of turning off the ringer, but simply because of the activities or noise going on around me. Then there are untimely calls where I choose to hit the silence button, intending to return the call at a more convenient time.

Is it possible that we do the same thing to God? I know there were times in past years when I "hit the silence button" and completely ignored God. Maybe it seemed as though the timing was bad or there would be a better time for me to "get serious" about God. The intention was always there, but later would be better, or so I thought—and just when exactly would that be? Sound familiar?

Even as Christians, sometimes we can miss God's call. Maybe not intentionally, but because of all the noise and activities around us, the voice of God is drowned out. Perhaps even we too hit the silence button on a call to serve, thinking later would be better.

In the book of Jeremiah, the Lord says, "Call to Me, and I will answer you, and I will tell you great and mighty things, which you do not know. Behold, I will bring to you health and healing, and I will heal you; and I will reveal to you an abundance of peace and truth" (Jeremiah 33:3, 6).

"The Lord is near to all who call upon Him, to all who call upon Him in truth" (Psalm 145:18).

The most important call of all is the call to follow Christ. Jesus said in John 14:6, "I am the way, and the truth and the life; no one comes to the Father but through Me." It is not enough to know only *about* Him; we must know Him personally, believing and receiving the work of Christ for ourselves.

God speaks to us anytime and anywhere. So what do we do? Do we hit the silence button, promising to call back at a more convenient time? Do we ignore the call altogether and miss any opportunity to bless and be blessed? We must be careful not to let daily distractions get in the way of hearing God's call.

Glory to God, the line also goes both ways, as we can call on God anytime and anywhere. There are no "right" times, for He is always available. Are you hearing the call of God? Now is the time to answer His call.

Most gracious Lord, thank you for all the ways in which You speak to us every day. Your Word tells us that when we draw near to You, You draw near to us. Help us to be mindful of the clutter in our lives that drown You out. Forgive us for the times when in our stubbornness or rebellion we have chosen to ignore You. Thank you for your patience and mercy. Restore us to the joy of Thy salvation and grant us a willing spirit to sustain us. In the blessed name of Jesus, amen.

Unmerited Favor

I have never been a huge fan of carnivals. The rides made me lose my lunch; the games made me lose my money. Nevertheless, while walking the fairway one county fair evening, my nephew and I decided to play one of the seemingly simpler games. For only two dollars, all we had to do was toss a golf ball into the hole of the center ring as many times as we could and watch our plastic pony cross the finish line. During a few practice throws, I found I was ridiculously uncoordinated at this game.

The starting bell sounded and the race was on. Toss after toss I laughed at the disgrace of my "skill" but continued with the game, recognizing I was a total failure. I glanced up at the tracks, expecting to see my lonely horse still in the starting gate, but amazingly, it was in the lead!

How did that happen? I hadn't put *one* ball in the hole to that point. Granted, the person to my left could hardly stay in his seat due to an over-consumption of *refreshments,* but my nephew seated on my right, as well as others, were making score after score.

Now, I am not so naïve to the fact that I had a little help somewhere. The carnie demonstrated his peculiar favor for me in that while I was yet a pathetic player, he nudged my pony to victory. I felt a little undeserving as I chose from the large stuffed animals lining the top shelf. Even so, I quietly walked away with a floppy, cross-eyed tiger.

As a child of God, we too find ourselves in a position of unworthiness, knowing that we do not deserve the rewards of heaven for the things we have done. My life proved to be try after failed try, leaving me feeling more and more a failure, recognizing I simply did not measure up to my own self-imposed religious standards.

All will soon discover that no matter how much practice, skill, or will we may possess, we prove ourselves pathetic players in the seemingly simple game of life. We look at our lives and consider ourselves still locked behind the gates of our spiritual inadequacies.

"But God demonstrates His own love for us in that while we were yet sinners, Christ died for us" (Romans 5:8).

There is not a thing we can do on our own to earn salvation. There are no hoops to jump, targets to hit, or swindling to arrange to secure a place in the kingdom. The price was paid over two thousand years ago as the Son of God said, "It is finished" and died on the cross at Calvary. "For God so loved the world that He gave His only begotten Son, that whoever believes in Him shall not perish but have eternal life" (John 3:16).

Jesus did not deserve the cross; we did. We do not deserve the gift of God's grace, but He gives to anyone who will receive.

"For it is by grace you have been saved through faith; and that not of yourselves, it is the gift of God; not as a result of works so that no one may boast" (Ephesians 2:8–9).

God's affection for us causes Him to reward us not just with eternal life but abundant life on earth, as well as a precious relationship with the King of kings and Lord of lords. Are we unworthy? Yes, but the offer still stands. Receive it in Jesus's name.

Blessed be our God, who has blessed us with every spiritual blessing in the heavenly places in Christ, that we would be holy and blameless before Him. Thank you Lord that even in our pathetic and wretched state, You died for us. Through Your Holy Spirit, we now live for You. To the King eternal, immortal, invisible, the only God, be honor and glory forever and ever. Amen.

Oh, Be Careful, Little Ears

If someone were to ask me to name something for which I have very deep convictions, it would have to be the influence of music in our lives. It has been said that "if one desires to know the condition of a kingdom, the quality of music will furnish the answer." I believe the same is true for the condition of an individual, a region, and a nation.

Have you ever noticed that the music found in the closets of the volatile youth involved in a horrific massacre is typically disturbingly dark and sinister? I have yet to hear of forensic officials discovering a hidden stack of MC Hammer or Backstreet Boys albums, considering them as a possible motivator.

We have all experienced, however, the power that music has over the human psyche, even when we least expect it. Each of us has been completely engrossed in another activity when a song comes through the overhead speakers of a store or restaurant and immediately carries us away to another time and place. Most of the songs remind us of good times in childhood, high school, or college years, while others may remind us of a sacred or even a painful moment in our lives. Many songs, however, will take us somewhere we no longer care to go.

When God cleaned my spiritual house several years ago, He immediately convicted me of the music I was listening too. Granted, I was only a *soft rock* listener, growing up with the Bee Gees, Barry Manilow, Boz Skaggs, but even those had a tendency to take me places I knew could only work to distract me from God's call.

I visited a Christian bookstore, where a clerk introduced me to the world of praise and worship. A few days later while searching the frequencies on the radio, I also discovered a local contemporary Christian station. There I was presented with a huge variety of not only uplifting, soul-stirring music, but also several great pastors and teachers of the truth of God's Word.

John 10:10 says, "The thief comes to steal and kill and destroy; I [Jesus] come that they may have life, and have it abundantly." As Christians, and as Christian parents, we fail to realize the potential damage that these thieves in the form of secular music can have in our lives and in the lives of our children. Over time, they can give the enemy a foothold in the door of our mind, heart, and soul.

James 4:4 presses us, saying, "Do you not know that friendship with the world is hostility toward God? Therefore, whoever wishes to be a friend of the world makes himself an enemy of God."

Although Christians still possess the freedom to be a friend with the world, worldly friendship can rob us of our sweet fellowship with God, short-circuiting the blessings of God, along with interrupting the counsel of God.

So should we not be more concerned about the music of which we listen? Oliver Wendell Holmes said, "Take a music bath once or twice a week for a few seasons, and you will find that it is to the soul what a water-bath is to the body."

I encourage you to take a Christian music bath for a season and see if your spirit doesn't begin to soar to new heights. Build upon your foundation the music that bolsters your faith and glorifies God. You will be surprised at how often God uses godly music to minister to your heart at just the right moment. You will be surprised as well at how often you will draw upon the words in your memory in order to minister to another.

Father, You are the original creator of music, but the enemy, the prince of darkness and king of counterfeit, has once again set out to deceive and destroy our relationship with You. Help us to recognize and root out anything that is not of You. Your Word tells us that You inhabit the praise of Your people. May the music to our ears and the meditation of our hearts be acceptable unto You. In Jesus's name, amen.

Some Assembly Required

Several months ago, I purchased an unassembled computer desk and side table for a home computer and printer. Reading the box before purchase, the "assembly required" paragraph did not alarm me. I had tackled other projects before, and unlike my husband, I do not feel the urge to forgo the instructions!

My heart sank, however, when I emptied the contents of the box onto the floor. Amid several flats of pressed and veneered surfaces was an assortment of small plastic bags, each holding tiny metal or plastic objects. There were nuts, bolts, screws, plastic ring thingies, and a funny shaped tool, of which I had no clue of its use, but it should tell me in the ... oh, here it is—the instruction sheet.

My eyes crossed as I read the parts page listing each metal, plastic, and almost wood object, labeled with nearly every letter of the alphabet. I held one object up to the picture, scrutinizing its likeness. Hours later, I felt as though I had slain the giant sitting at my new, slightly shaky variation of a computer desk, and like the cat with its latest kill, I could not wait for my husband to return home.

When it comes to our personal faith, could it be that the average person feels about the way I felt when I dumped that box of scattered, unknown parts onto the floor. Has the church's evolvement over time led to the appearance of presenting so many odd-shaped formalities and veneered religious rituals that the world in which Jesus came to seek and save is cross-eyed from the numerous diverse elements?

British journalist and Christian writer Malcomb Muggeridge said, "Jesus did not come into the world to found a Church but to proclaim a Kingdom—the two being by no means the same thing."

As a baby Christian, I know I felt overwhelmed by what seemed to be an unending list of do's and don'ts, confused by the differences of denominations, pressed to memorize Scripture and attend Sunday services. My mind froze when opening the pages of Scripture, not knowing where to begin.

Then I crossed paths with a precious woman of God whose life radiated the light of Christ. She reminded me of the role of the Holy Spirit in my life and shared of the simplicity of following Christ. It was not about getting all the parts lined out and memorized. It was simply about knowing Christ fully, loving Him completely, and serving Him wholly. She explained that my faith was the creation of God's regenerating spirit working in me and not that of my own clever compilation. I walked away with a new awareness that I was one of God's prized projects.

I learned that day that I had held to an artificial image for years that in no way resembled the relationship to which God was calling me; the one to which God calls each of us. Beloved, our life in Christ is not about some shiny exterior of surface religiosity. It is a genuine, internal relationship with the living God.

"But the Kingdom of God is ... righteousness and peace and joy in the Holy Spirit" (Romans 14:17). The kingdom of God is an experience. It is a personal encounter with the pure love of God the Father, the Son, and Holy Spirit. Attempting to assemble and adhere to an itemized collection of man-made religious ideas, principles or traditions will provide nothing more than a substandard and shaky foundation for an artificial faith.

Christ prayed to the Father for all believers, saying, "The glory which You have given Me I have given to them, that they may be one, just as We are one; I in them and You in Me, that they may be perfected in unity, so that the world may know that You sent Me, and loved them, even as You loved Me" (John 17:22–23).

It seems so trivial now, but at the time, I could not wait to show my husband that "I" had single-handedly assembled that entire box of assorted parts into one complete unit. When we consider, however, the work that the God of all creation has done in us, for us, and through us, perhaps a proper response for the believer is to let the world know that "Christ is before all things and in Him all things hold together" (Colossians 1:17).

You, child of God, are His prized project.

God of the universe and keeper of our hearts, we are thankful for the opportunity to gather each week in our desired places of worship, however, may we never permit church to become a substitute for our relationship with Christ. Reassemble our hearts, Lord, to radiate an attitude of worship and praise, and renew a steadfast spirit within us. Perfect us together as one, Father, just as You, the Son, and Holy Spirit are one, that the world may see and know that You have loved them even as You loved Jesus. Amen.

Refining the Gift

I have heard that success is not measured simply by the abilities you possess; but rather, it is measured by *what you do* with those God-given abilities.

Each of us is born with what we call natural talents, gifts, or skills. Unique abilities are given us to either use or squander. Developing and honing natural talents while discovering ways to earn accolades or even income generally is considered as personal success. Discovering our God-given talents, honing them over time, and then using them in a way that pleases God and works to expand the family of God is called ministry.

Have you ever had a passionate desire to serve the Lord with your unique abilities, but your inconsistent faith walk or even blemished past arrests your aspirations for fear you will not be given credence in your ministry? Welcome to the family of God!

The beauty of God's Word is that all through the Bible God uses imperfect people to bring about His perfect plan. God is not looking for perfect people. He is looking for people whose hearts He can use. I am sure you have heard the expression, "He's not looking for ability; He's looking for availability." God takes the shattered pieces of our lives and refashions us to work out the defects, making us perfect in His image.

I love the imagery from the book of Jeremiah of the master potter. As the potter fashions the vessel, he can choose to either remove the imperfections or leave them as part of the beauty and individuality of the design. It is what makes the creation unique.

We find another vivid allegory in Malachi 3:3, stating, "He will sit as a refiner and purifier of silver" (NIV).

It is said when silver is refined, as the refiner holds the silver in the fire, he never leaves his work. He must keep his eye on the silver at all times in order that the intense fire might not destroy it. He skims off the dross, or valueless scum, from the silver, which rises to the surface under the extreme heat. The more dross removed, the clearer his image becomes in the surface of the silver. Isn't that a beautiful picture of what He does with us?

If you feel God leading you to employ a gift He has given you, I encourage you to step out in faith and know that He will meet you there when you do. Stay in the Word and continue to develop your relationship with the Giver of all gifts. Stay up, pray up, and lay up your treasures in heaven that nothing and no one can destroy!

Be mindful however that there will be workers of iniquity who thrive on trying to bring you down by reminding you of your past stumbling blocks or failures. That is the attack of the enemy. If you have never been under attack, chances are you have never really been a threat to the domain of darkness. Jesus was ridiculed, scorned, and beaten. Why should we expect better treatment than He received?

We soon discover that the world's standard of "success" comes up short when compared to what God is able to do with even the smallest of talents in His faithful ones. "Whoever can be trusted with very little can also be trusted with much" (Luke 16:10a NIV).

Whatever gift God has given, though ours for a time, remains the property of God. We have been granted only the use of it, under the direction of our Lord, to glorify our Father in heaven. All glory, honor, power, and praise belong to our great God!

Father, we thank you for every opportunity to serve You. We pray for those who seek and follow Your guidance, allowing You to work through them to accomplish Your purpose. May Your spirit stir their heart with a divine boldness, empowering them with the gifts You have given. Thank you for finding us worthy of ministering through and remind us often that "greater is He who is in me, than he who is in the world." In Jesus's name, amen.

Daze of Confusion

I recently received one of those dreaded middle-of-the-night phone calls. At three thirty in the morning, my cell phone rang. In mid-dream confusion, I brought the phone close to my blurry, astigmatic eyes and read a number I did not recognize. Immediately, I shifted into panic mode. In the time it took for me to open my phone to answer, my mind had already raced down the phobic path of fear and trepidation. It was a classic case of imaginations run amok.

It turned out to be a wrong number; someone speaking broken English was checking on a ride to the airport! Satisfied there was no crisis, I could put my mind at ease. The problem was that while my mind was at ease, my body surely was not. I was now wide-awake, accompanied by a stomachache and throbbing calves, the side effects of surplus adrenaline. By divine design, adrenaline is a wonderful partner for bodily threats, emergencies, and even personal challenges, but at three thirty in the morning, it is a nuisance.

Ironically, what had set the stage for my immediate panic mode was a conversation that took place earlier that evening. My daughter had called from the cruise ship on which she and her fiancé's family were vacationing in Mexico. She was quite sick. Although she had received medical attention, the fact that she was so far away instilled a level of anxiety in me of which only a mother can empathize.

I went to bed that evening and took my concerns to the Lord. I adamantly believed for her safety and health, as well as my peace, and drifted off into sweet sleep. Then, a few hours later the phone call came, and in a sleepy and shaken stupor, I *impulsively assumed* the foreign number was an emergency call placed from the ship.

As Christians, we are reminded frequently that we are to "walk by faith and not by sight" (or feelings). This is one of the most difficult areas in which believers struggle. We struggle not because of a "hyper hormone" but rather a manic mind, most often out of fear of the unknown.

Well, what exactly is faith, if we are to walk by it?

"Now faith is the assurance of things hoped for, the conviction of things not seen ... and without faith it is impossible to please God, for he who comes to God must believe that He is a rewarder of those who seek Him" (Hebrews 11:1, 6).

So what harm can fear really do anyway?

"The fear of man brings a snare, but he who trusts in the Lord will be exalted" (Prov. 29:25).

But I think I can handle this problem on my own; I don't really need to bother God with this one.

"Trust in the Lord with all your heart and do not lean on your own understanding … and do not be wise in your own eyes" (Prov. 3:5, 7).

"Therefore humble yourselves under the mighty hand of God, that He may exalt you at the proper time, casting all your anxiety on Him, because He cares for you" (1 Peter 5:6–7).

When life catches us off guard, we find ourselves at first in a daze of confusion. Often, our initial reaction is out of fear and panic, drawing all sorts of irrational conclusions. Almighty God, however, is not a God of confusion but of peace (1 Cor. 14:33). Learning to seek Him in those manic moments will lead us to the peace that surpasses all comprehension, to guard our hearts and minds in Christ Jesus. (Phil. 4:7)

Furthermore, the Bible warns to "be of sober spirit, be on the alert. Your adversary, the devil, prowls about like a roaring lion, seeking someone to devour" (1 Peter 5:8).

Yet take heart, because "the eyes of the Lord move to and fro throughout the earth that He may strongly support those whose heart is completely His" (2 Chronicles 16:9).

While the devil is on the prowl, the eyes of Almighty God are constantly in motion to send whatever support is necessary in our time of need. The more we learn to trust the Lord in our circumstances, and acknowledge Him in all our ways, the more we will be able to relax, knowing that all power in heaven and earth are in His hands.

Faith comes by hearing, and hearing, by the word of God. As we hear and speak the truth of God's Word by faith in all our circumstances, we will begin to see our thoughts and responses line up with His Word. With our mind, body, and spirit in sync, walking by faith becomes more graceful, more resolute, and more courageous.

But, cut yourself some slack at three thirty in the morning.

Blessed Father, we thank you that the evidence of Your goodness surrounds us every day. Though we may not see the reasons for our circumstance right now, we can be assured that all things work together for good for those who love You and are called according to Your purpose. Help us to remain firm in our faith, knowing that we have all the support of heaven. In Jesus's name, amen.

Deliver Us from Evil

My sister lives in a residential area surrounding a beautiful pond. On one end of the pond is a dense and colorful grove of trees, providing a charming backdrop for the lively, sparkling water. The pond, fully stocked with fish, a congregation of amusing ducks, and other assorted species of God's amazing creatures, offers free entertainment, especially when His most clever creature, the human, attempts to interact with nature.

One day, while enjoying the coolness of late afternoon from her back patio, she noticed a couple at the end of the pond near the dense trees. The woman was standing at the water's edge while her husband waded out into waist-high water, reaching carefully toward a low-hanging branch. My sister had observed this couple fishing on numerous occasions and assumed he was trying to loosen a tangled line caught in the tree.

After a few minutes, she looked again to find the

man now in shallower water, but crouching down with both hands beneath the water, walking v-e-r-y slowly, this time *toward* the bank. The woman looked rather concerned, so my sister decided to ask if they needed any assistance, to which they both abruptly snapped, *"No!"*

Minutes later, the woman appeared at my sister's sliding glass door. She was in need of a grocery bag. My sister asked the standard question: "Paper or plastic?" It did not matter—just something to hold a *snake!* The woman casually proceeded to inform my sister that a snake had bitten her husband and as a precaution, wanted to take the snake with them to the emergency room!

The next day, the couple was again fishing at the pond. Curiosity consumed my sister, so she asked how they were doing following the excitement of the previous evening. The man responded positively and continued to fill in all the blanks about the incident.

Apparently, he had indeed snagged his line in the tree. In his attempt to free his line, he spotted a snake near his entangled lure. The man tried very carefully not to disturb the snake; however, the snake elected to defend his domain aggressively, biting the man's hand, latching on tightly.

Thinking quickly (hmmm, that's questionable), the man grabbed the affixed snake and held it underwater in hopes of drowning the snake so that it would release. (Do you have chills?)

Now, I am not certain of the cost of a new lure, but I have feeling a trip to the hospital ER costs much more than a fishing lure. But you know what they say about hindsight.

Since the Garden of Eden, the schemes of the devil have not changed. Satan lies in wait for each of us, looking for opportunities to snag us in our faith walk. No matter how much we rationalize, getting too close to evil practically ensures an imminent strike. The word of God instructs us to be on the lookout, but also to *avoid* even the appearance of evil.

"But examine everything carefully; hold fast to that which is good; abstain from every form of evil" (1 Thess. 5:21–22).

The Spirit of God will alert us when we are wading into dangerous territory and will always provide a way of escape. "But with the temptation will provide the way of escape ... " (1 Cor. 10:13). It is up to us to listen and respond wisely and obediently. Failure to do so will result in suffering and grief, a painful lesson learned the hard way!

Our heavenly Father, Your name is so holy and sacred. Come and establish Your kingdom on earth so that it will be just as it is in heaven. Bless us with our daily needs and forgive us for our sins, as we also forgive those who sin against us. Let us not yield to temptation and deliver us out of evil's schemes, for the kingdom, the power, and the glory are Yours forever and ever! Amen.

Me and My Shadow

"Me and my shadow" is an endearing term used to label best friends, mother and daughter, father and son, as well as a host of other close relationships. For years, I felt as if I would trip over my young daughter if I turned around too quickly. Grandparents with a third-generation shadow are the most precious.

Children from every generation most likely have played the "shadow game," where the object was to stay inside the shadow of someone nearby, preferably an adult since they cast a larger shadow. Being inside the shadow was the safe zone. These were the images that came to mind as I recently read from Psalm 91.

"He who dwells in the shelter of the Most High, will rest in the shadow of the Almighty" (Psalm 91:1 NIV).

The entire chapter is so beautiful and captures the essence of the safety and security found in trusting Almighty God. Whether Psalm 91 is a continuation of the previous chapter written by Moses or a psalm possibly written by David, it is a powerful psalm of encouragement to believers, ending with the promise from God of blessings, honor, and a long, satisfying life.

To *dwell* refers to residing, inhabiting, settling, and staying. It is not a temporary visit, a Sunday morning drop-in, or stopover. It is a daily place of protection from the elements as well as comfort and a place of complete rest.

"I will say to the Lord, 'My refuge and my fortress; my God in whom I trust!' He will cover you with His feathers, and under His wings you will find refuge" (Psalms 91:2–4 ESV). "For He will command His angels concerning you, to guard you in all your ways" (Psalm 91:11 ESV).

The "shelter of the most high" is available to all but reached by few. Some have had a glimpse of it, others have had a temporary experience, but it is the call of God and a life lived in His grace, bringing about the obedience of faith that we find ourselves continually in this place.

Jesus echoed the psalm as He lamented over Jerusalem. "Jerusalem, Jerusalem! How often I wanted to gather your children … the way a hen gathers her chicks under her wings, and you were unwilling" (Matthew 23:37).

Our young children have no trouble in clinging to us for safety and security. They know instinctively where to run to for shelter. Jesus reminds us that we are to "become like children" if we are to enter the kingdom of heaven.

Love the Lord your God with all your heart, soul, mind, and strength as you dwell in the shelter of the most high. Worship and adore Him daily. Praise Him for who He is regardless of your circumstances. Rest in knowing that the angels of God have been given divine orders to watch over you.

A life lived in obedience to God is a life lived in the shadow and shelter of the Lord. If we find ourselves outside of the shadow, outside of the safe zone, it is not because God moved. We give up that protection when we choose to step outside of His will (or shadow) and do things our own way.

"As the mountains surround Jerusalem, so the Lord surrounds His people" (Psalm 125:2). We thank you, Father, for the complete rest that comes from abiding daily in You. Help us to cease from our own works and to let You take over every area of our lives. In Your shadow, Father, we can be still and know that You are God.

Hide and Seek

Forrest Gump was *the* movie of great one-liners in the 90s. My favorite came from Lieutenant Dan the night the New Year's celebration turned bad. Following an outrage of pent-up anger and disappointment at his lot in life, he turned to Forrest and said, "Have you found Jesus yet, Gump?"

Forrest jerked his head in surprise and replied, "I didn't know I was supposed to be looking for him, sir."

From time to time, we hear the declaration urging us to "seek the Lord," and perhaps like Gump, many may think to themselves, *I didn't know I was supposed to be looking for Him.*

So what does it mean really to "seek the Lord"?

Go back to the Garden of Eden. After Adam and Eve had partaken of the forbidden fruit and recognized their nakedness, they attempted to cover themselves, as well as hide from God.

God said, "Adam, where are you?" (Genesis 3:9).

It was not that *God* did not know where Adam

was. God wanted *Adam* to know where Adam was. More exact, He wanted Adam to acknowledge his rebellion, and Adam did what many do—he blamed someone else.

It is man's nature to hide from God before he ever considers seeking Him. God seeks us first, that we might see and know where we are. Like Adam, man tries to hide, cover, make excuses, and blame someone else for sin. God wants to cover us.

In the garden, God covered Adam and Eve with animal skin that required the sacrifice of an animal. On the cross, He covered us by the shed blood of His beloved Son. The call of God is as loud today as it was in the garden.

"Where are you?"

Our future lies in the response given to that question. It seems only when we are drowning in our sin that we then become seekers of mercy, deliverance, and forgiveness. It is this type of seeking that prepares the lost to receive the salvation of God.

Just as a parent rushes to the side of an injured or sick child, God rushes to our side when we acknowledge our sin—when we cry out to Him in our distress (Psalm 103:13). He seeks us in our shame and desires to cover us in His righteousness, wrapping us in the mercy and grace of the Father.

"I sought the Lord and He answered, and delivered me from all my fears ... How blessed is the man who takes refuge in Him" (Psalm 34:4, 8b).

God is the original seeker. Jesus came to seek and save that which was lost (Luke 19:10), and where mercy and sorrow meet, grace abounds. Once we partake of God's amazing grace and abounding love, our heart's desire will be to know Him even more. We then will yearn to seek His face and not just His hand, loving Him for more than just His benefits, crying out for God this time with hearts that hunger for truth and righteousness. The degree of our hunger determines the degree of our searching.

Be ever attentive to where you are in your walk with God, examining yourselves often to see if you are acting in faith or in the flesh. "Test yourselves to see if you are in the faith; examine yourselves! Or do you not recognize this about yourselves, that Jesus Christ is in you—unless indeed you fail the test?" (2 Cor. 13:5)

Jesus said, "Seek and you shall find" (Matthew 7:7). God desires us to seek Him, but He sought us before we sought Him, to crown us with loving kindness and compassion and to satisfy our years (Psalms 103:4–5). May we forever devote our hearts and souls to seeking Him.

Father, Your Word says "for as high as the heavens are above the earth, so great is Your love toward us." But all I know, Father, is *"I once was lost and now am found; was blind but now I see."* Thank you for finding us just as we were that you might cover us in your merciful love. Hallelujah to the Lamb of God!

Casual Casualties

A modern trend in business today is "casual Friday." Its origin is uncertain, but one theory behind its initiation was so that employees could show their support and enthusiasm of upcoming ballgames. Perhaps for others, its purpose was to exhibit a more relaxed and stress-free atmosphere. Many welcomed the dress-down day; others were skeptical.

As the concept evolved, each with their own perception of casual, some employers began to change their views of the laid-back proposal. A few companies were experiencing the high cost of casual Friday, as a lax performance seemed to accompany their casual dress.

Likewise, a high cost also comes, not with the casual *dress* of Christians, but rather with the casual *commitment*. Why is it that if at least 90 percent of Americans claim to believe in God and nearly one hundred million Americans are either members or attend worship services, that the church isn't making a greater moral or spiritual impact on society?

We can point fingers at the rebellion of the sixties, the confusion of the seventies, the selfish yuppie mentality of the eighties, the Internet of the nineties, or even the self-absorption of Hollywood, as to the decadence and depravity of our nation and threat to Christianity. The greatest threat to the church, however, does not come from the outside but rather from among its own members. It is a little word called *apathy,* also known as "casual Christianity."

It has been said, "All that is necessary for the triumph of evil is for good men to do nothing." The dictionary defines *apathy* as a lack of concern, laziness, lethargy, indifference, or boredom. These could be the very reasons many people avoid the church.

Sadly, many of God's people make a decision to receive Christ as Savior but then refuse to follow and serve Him as Lord. They desire forgiveness, salvation, and eternity in heaven yet are living defeated and unfruitful lives. One pastor labeled that type of decision as "Fire Insurance."

In Revelation 3:15–16, Jesus says to the Church of Laodicea, "I know your deeds that you are neither cold nor hot; I wish that you were either cold or hot. So because you are lukewarm, and neither hot nor cold, will I spit you out of My mouth."

These are admonishing words from our Lord to those who wear the name of Christ but bear little resemblance to Him. The Amen, the faithful and true Witness, the beginning of the creation of God, is issuing a wake-up call to a sleeping church. He says,

You say, "I am rich. I have everything I want. I don't need a thing!" And you don't realize that you are wretched and miserable and poor and blind and naked. So I advise you to buy gold from me—gold that has been purified by fire. Then you will be rich. Also, buy white garments from Me so you will not be shamed by your nakedness, and ointment for your eyes so you will be able to see.

Revelation 3:17–18 NLT

Jesus was saying that many appear to have it all figured out spiritually and need nothing from anyone and are oblivious to the fact that, spiritually, they were as blind beggars, threadbare and homeless. He beckons them to purchase from Him true wealth, heavenly garments, and salve to anoint the eyes so they may see clearly.

Jesus's somber words are spoken in love for His children. He disciplines those whom He loves and is holding them accountable. Jesus is not impressed with church attendance. What He longs for is a personal relationship with you and with me, even if it is the second (or third) time around. "Come back" is all that He asks.

"Behold, I stand at the door and knock; if anyone hears My voice and opens the door, I will come in to him and dine with him, and he with Me" (Revelation 3:20).

In this verse, Jesus is speaking to the church, not to those outside the church as this scripture is often used. Jesus is calling the casual, halfhearted Christian back to a place of divine fellowship with Him, with whole-hearted love and devotion.

There is nothing better than kicking off the heels, loosening the tie, and putting on our favorite blue jeans or sweats. We all love to be comfortable and casual. The casualness we all cherish so much is quite suitable for some places of business, our homes, shopping, and even in our churches.

However, when it comes to honoring the God of all creation, the King eternal, immortal, invisible, the only God our Savior, the One who went to the cross for your sin and mine, then perhaps our aim should not be to see how comfortable or casual we can be in our faith. God was never casual in His love for us, so should we be so casual in our love for Him?

Father, we don't want to live a casual Christian life. Forgive us for taking our eyes off You and setting our eyes upon the world. We know, Lord, that we can never know true living when we exchange Your truth for lies. May we never be casual in our relationship with You. We hear You knocking, Lord. Come in and be Lord over every area of our lives, for You alone are worthy. In Jesus's name, amen.

A Pleasant Aroma

My sister is a fragrance aficionada. It is unusual for her to purchase the same fragrance year after year. She loves to sample the latest scents and does not bother with off-the-shelf eau de toilette. I can seldom pronounce the names of most of the perfumes adorning her bathroom shelf. She lives simply; this is just one area she chooses to splurge a bit.

What is it about perfumes and colognes that strongly appeals to most human sensory receptors? Manufacturers create fragrances from the most delicate of bouquets, to the rough and tumble woodsy scents, to the ever-popular musky aromas. Musk always brings back memories of cologne-clouded dressing rooms in high school.

Proverbs tells us "oil and perfume make the heart glad" (Prov. 27:9). Fragrance designers attempt to tap into all areas of the human psyche as they experiment in high-tech labs. There is definitely a science involved in the designer's creations, but bottom line, nearly everyone loves a pleasant aroma!

In the Old Testament, Scripture speaks of sacrifices being a pleasant aroma before the Lord. The sacrifices then were typically an animal burnt offering. I don't know about you, but I find the smell of anything burning, other than a candle, rather offensive, but the Lord called it a pleasant aroma.

The sacrifices of the Old Testament of course typified Christ and were a demonstration of communion, devotion, and worship to God. The aroma of true worship pleases our holy God. Though we no longer have a need to practice sacrificial burnt offerings, the Lord still distinguishes between the pleasant aroma of pure worship and the stench of empty religion and vain worship.

I love the heart of King David. When Nathan confronted David about his sin with Bathsheba, David knew it was not simply a matter of a ritualistic ceremony of sacrifice but a matter of the heart.

"For Thou dost not delight in sacrifice, otherwise I would give it; Thou art not pleased with burnt offering. The sacrifices of God are a broken spirit; A broken and contrite heart, O God, Thou wilt not despise" (Psalms 51:16–17). David was still known as "a man after God's own heart."

The Apostle Paul said, "But thanks be to God, who always leads us in His triumphs in Christ, and manifests through us the sweet aroma of the knowledge of Him in every place. For we are a fragrance of Christ to God among those who are being saved and among those who are perishing; to the one an aroma from death to death, to the other an aroma of life to life" (2 Corinthians 2:14–16).

God's gift to us is eternal life through His Son, as well as abundant life on earth. The first step in pleasing Him is our faith in Him. Our sweet-smelling gift to Him is a heart of pure worship—holy, acceptable, and pleasing in His sight.

Holy Lord, we thank you for providing a way for us to commune with the God of all creation. May our worship be pure, acceptable, and pleasing unto You. Help us to see that worship is more about the heart rather than lip service or sacrifice. We pray that in both corporate and private moments of worship, that You be high and lifted up in all our praise, glory, and honor, because You, O Lord, are worthy.

Hooked on a Feeling

One of the most fulfilling moments God can bring into our day is the opportunity to minister to one who is searching for purpose and truth. Whether they be an unbeliever or one who is "sitting the fence," it is an opportunity to share what God has given to us with another that could ultimately change his or her life. There is no greater reward than to see the light of Christ shine in the eyes of a new believer.

I once had the occasion to speak with an individual who admitted to "sitting the fence" for twenty or more years. Claiming to believe, yet unwilling to receive, the hesitancy was the result of one minor holdup: the feeling of awkwardness.

If you've spent much time in church at all, you've undoubtedly heard of the analogy used to describe faith, as the blindfolded person falls backward into the promised arms of one positioned safely behind him. Falling backward while blindfolded *is* an awkward feeling. It is counter to our natural balance, and we instinctively want to catch ourselves or flail our arms.

My first time on snow skis was indeed a moment of awkwardness. My high school classmates can testify to that. By the way, did I mention it was my last time?

Certainly, several medical examinations are awkward, leaving you feeling somewhat violated, but are necessary for the diagnosis of health issues or maintaining ongoing treatments. Even witnessing to others can feel awkward, especially the first few times.

In other words, awkwardness is a part of life, but it should never keep us from trying new things, maintaining our health, ministering to others, and for sure, never keep us out of heaven. Usually the cure for awkwardness is simple—trust, practice, and patience. Other times, it may require deeper investigation.

Have you ever noticed that sin can be so much more comfortable than righteousness? At least, that is, in our natural state. The flesh tends to hunger for things of the flesh. The spirit hungers for things of the Spirit. When sin is uncomfortable, you will know the Spirit has taken up residence in your heart. If sin is easy and fun, it is time for a spiritual checkup.

The Bible encourages us to "trust in the Lord with all your heart, and lean not on your own understanding, but in all your ways acknowledge Him and He will make your paths straight" (Proverbs 3:5–6).

What I love about this scripture is that we can not only trust Him to straighten our future paths, but we can also trust Him to straighten the crooked and twisted paths of our past, giving us a clearer understanding of the things that held us captive, which hooked us to feelings of insecurity, fear, or worthlessness.

The body of Christ plays a key role in the first steps of the new believer. The encouragement we offer imparts courage and strength, as well as direction in the new life, and is vitally important in the early stages. Proverbs 15:23b says, "How delightful is the timely word."

I've heard it said that "the voice of God is the Father, the face of God is Jesus, the breath of God is the Holy Spirit, and the hand of God is the Church." God uses you and me to encourage new believers as the Spirit of God draws them to His side.

I gently pressed the individual that day to understand more about the awkward feeling. I soon discovered there were much deeper issues responsible for the feelings of awkwardness. God was already at work, as the timeliness of His Word began to melt away years of hurt and fear, softening a hardened heart.

Hebrews 11:6 reminds us, "Without faith, it is impossible to please God…and He rewards those who earnestly seek Him." God always responds to the searching heart.

Perhaps you are one who is "sitting the fence" or feeling awkward about stepping out in faith. Be encouraged to know that if you are at least thinking about it, it means that the irresistible grace of God is gently drawing you. If unsure of your next move, seek the assistance of a mature believer who will delight in leading you into the throne room of God. I have a *feeling* He is waiting for you.

Holy God, You are God of our past, present, and future—the same yesterday, today, and forever. For those who are struggling with receiving You by faith, Lord, we pray You prepare their hearts as You send Your chosen one with a timely word that offers hope and truth. We walk by faith and not by sight or feelings. May feelings never prevent us from ministering or keep us from You. In Jesus's name, amen.

Enemy Territory

One evening, my sister and I sat on her patio watching a young couple across the pond playing with a pair of Labrador retrievers along the grassy bank. Suddenly, one of the dogs took in after a duck that was sunning itself at the edge of the bank. Immediately the duck scrambled toward the water and swam a safe distance out. The young Lab followed with reckless abandon, paddling with all he had, while the duck appeared to propel away effortlessly.

The clever duck, more comfortable in its watery surroundings, would occasionally disappear under the water. It had quickly become obvious that what began as a game of chase for the dog had now turned into a devious game of hide and seek for the duck, as the feathery foe would dip and then pop up several yards away, taunting the dog repeatedly.

We watched as the dog, now exhausted and confused, began to sink lower and lower in the water as his strength and stamina waned. Previously confident and secure on dry land, the dog now floundered in the depths of enemy territory. Appearing increasingly vulnerable, the defeated dog eventually was able to paddle his way back to the shore.

Simon Peter made the mistake of tempting fate in enemy territory. Peter, so confident and secure when he was with Jesus, promised never to disown Him. We know that very night, he denied Jesus three times after entering the courtyard of those who arrested Him.

It is a common scenario for believers as we too find ourselves sinking deeper and deeper when we enter territory opposed to God's will. Teen believers contend they can party with their peers as long as they wear a cross around their neck. Believing singles assume they can date or even marry a nonbeliever in the hopes of changing them one day. We rationalize our entertainment, our habits, or even hobbies as not being "that big of a deal," and we let down our guard, giving Satan a foothold.

Peter thought his faith was strong enough to handle any temptation and was found caught off guard as he warmed himself by the fire. We do the same. We may not see the consequences as quickly as Peter did, but they eventually will surface. It is impossible to sit at the devil's fire and not get burned.

I love the quote by Pastor E. Ray Jones. He said, "We have a tendency to overestimate our ability to cope with temptation and underestimate our ability to cope with suffering."

First Corinthians 10:12 states "If you think you

are standing firm, be careful not to fall" (NIV). Most often, what we consider our greatest strength will ultimately trip us up simply because in our overconfidence, we let down our guard.

The good news is we serve a God of second (and third) chances. Jesus restored Simon Peter for every time he denied Him by asking, "Peter, do you love me?" Peter replied, "Lord, you know I love you." Jesus said, "Then feed my sheep" (John 21:17 NIV), essentially a statement of ordination.

Just as the duck lured the gullible Labrador into hazardous territory, Satan also attempts to lure us blindly into unsettling surroundings. His sole purpose is always to confuse and disorient as panic and fear slowly drain every ounce of our strength.

"But whatever is born of God overcomes the world; and this is the victory that has overcome the world—our faith" (1 John 5: 4).

Hallelujah, failure is never final! The Bible is full of people who have fallen, have been restored and used of God in a mighty way. Just as Jesus fully restored Peter, giving him the keys to the kingdom, He will restore us for every time we have fallen.

Lord, in quiet confidence, we come before Your throne, knowing that there we will find the mercy and grace for our individual circumstance. Forgive us for the times we have failed You. Strengthen and restore us as we worship You in spirit and in truth. Remind us that failure is never final but oftentimes a springboard for Your sovereign plan. In Jesus's name, amen.

The Day Before

Only a few today will be able to describe where they were and what they were doing the day of President Kennedy's assassination. A later generation will recall the day of the Space Shuttle Challenger disaster. Even more will remember vividly the day of the Murrah Building bombing and most recent, the moment terrorists shook America's foundation of safety, destroying the World Trade Centers.

However, do you remember what you were doing the day *before?* Odd question, I know. Most certainly, it is not the common question. Some, I am sure, have a particular personal event cementing the day before in their minds. For most, however, it was business as usual—going to work, getting the kids to school, planning parties, attending meetings, etc.

Have you noticed that it seems only when disasters occur we automatically shift into another frame of mind? We become more aware of our surroundings, more compassionate with our neighbor, perhaps even more self-disciplined. Disasters cause us to reestablish our priorities, reminding us of our mortality and of how fallible and temporary we are. It usually lasts only as long as the media broadcasts the chaos. Then it is business as usual all over again. Alas, the change was only temporary.

Time, experience, and education can prepare us somewhat for our readiness and reaction to the unexpected, but what of our attentiveness and reaction to *expected* events? The answer to that question depends solely upon one's belief, perception, and understanding of the anticipated event. *How one believes determines how one responds!*

Before the Great Flood, people bustled about, eating and drinking, going to work, walking the saber-tooth, catching a great pantomime, listening to "rock" music, and texting on stone tablets. They had no idea of what was coming or of what was to come. Noah most likely tried to warn them, but they perceived him as foolish, turning their backs to the ark. The clouds came, the thunder clapped, and the Lord shut the door to the ark. Noah's family was safe, but not so for those outside of the ark, caught up in the ways of the world.

In Luke 17, the Pharisees questioned Jesus about the coming kingdom of God foretold by the prophets. Jesus told them, "Behold, the kingdom of God is in your midst" (verse 20). As usual, the Pharisees missed it. He was telling them they did not need to look for any future signs; the kingdom of God was already there, standing close enough to touch. So close and yet so far.

Jesus then turned to His disciples, who fully grasped the present kingdom but had questions about the future. He encouraged them, however, not to chase after those claiming to "look here" or "look there." He then proceeded in their interest telling them, "And just as it happened in the days of Noah, so it shall be also in the days of the Son of Man: they were eating, they were drinking, they were marrying, they were being given in marriage, until the day that Noah entered the ark, and the flood came and destroyed them all" (Luke 17:26–27).

The kingdom of God remains in our midst through the Holy Spirit. "And He will guide you into all truth … and He will show you things to come" (John 16:13.) Just as Noah and his family entered the ark by faith, we too enter the kingdom by faith. He who has ears to hear, let him hear. Those who are not born again cannot see the kingdom of God.

Our present days are indeed like the days of Noah. Let us not grow complacent in our activities. We must be about our Father's business. "Straighten up and lift up your heads, because your redemption is drawing near" (Luke 21:28).

Often, in the face of great disaster, change is only temporary. Allow God to use every resource available in preparing you to remain dedicated and determined in making the necessary changes and preparations for you or your family. Utilize disaster as a means to strengthen you, forever increasing your faith.

Today is the "day before" whatever happens tomorrow. What if the Lord returns tomorrow? Where will you be? Where will your family be? The blessing of the "day before" is that it offers an opportunity to prepare for tomorrow. Today is the day of salvation. Today is the day of decision.

Jesus is the ark of our salvation, and all who enter will be saved. The Son of God is returning soon. Are you on board?

Eternal Father, we thank you for Jesus, who is our salvation and for the Holy Spirit—Your kingdom come to earth. May Your will be done in our hearts today, Lord, as You establish Your kingdom of righteousness within us. May we continually be on guard, praying at all times for strength to endure the days, while living in faith-filled expectation of our coming King. In Jesus's name, amen.

Where's Jesus?

Years ago, when the kids were small, Sunday mornings became something of a well-orchestrated exercise. It took two vehicles to get five people to church. I left early with my young daughter to set up for my Sunday school class, and my husband trailed a few minutes behind with the boys. After the service, we usually left in reverse order.

Following one Sunday morning service, I stayed behind arranging my classroom for something later in the week. My husband informed me he was going to take the kids home. I packed up my things only a minute or two behind my husband and headed for the house.

Pulling in behind him in the driveway, I noticed the boys already playing with the dog but did not see our five-year-old daughter. My husband walked toward me with a jokey smirk on his face, while I sported the same.

"Where's Kaci?" he teasingly asked.

Thinking she had ducked down in the seat of his pickup, I answered, "Well...I don't know? Where *is* Kaci?"

We exchanged this playful banter for only a couple more rounds, until it suddenly turned more somber.

"Seriously, where *is* Kaci?" we both anxiously inquired.

Immediately, I was sick to my stomach, realizing what we had done. My husband thought she had stayed with me; I thought she had gone with him. I raced back down to the church, expecting to find her little face and hands plastered to the glass of the front door of a locked church, screaming. Instead, she was calmly helping a dear woman empty the communion trays, but I still felt like we were the world's worst parents.

I wonder if that is how Jesus's parents felt when they learned they had left Jesus behind in Jerusalem (Luke 2:43). Most likely, in the bustle of the feast and the crowd of people, they assumed Jesus surely was with someone in the large traveling group. It would be three days before they reunited with Jesus; it was only three minutes before I found my daughter. They found Jesus in the temple speaking with the elders and teachers; I found my daughter in the kitchen sipping down surplus communion cups.

Have you ever wondered how Mary and Joseph could have possibly left Jesus, the Son of God, behind? How could they have traveled for so long before missing Him, but do we not do that ourselves?

How often have we become so engrossed in the

acceleration of our hectic lives that we really had not thought that much about Jesus for several days? It is easy to forego personal Bible study or Scripture reading because of a busy schedule, assuring ourselves that we will get back on track as soon as things settle down. Then we find an excuse to miss one Sunday service, then two ... and three.

Perhaps we temporarily neglect our calling and leave the responsibility of keeping track of Jesus to a spouse or Sunday school teacher, assuming He surely is with him or her. Focusing on ourselves rather than on God, and without consistent godly influence, we begin to slip back into old habits and behaviors. Eventually, almost without notice, old temptations arise and we fall back into a past sin. Finally, in a moment of chaos and panic, we recognize that we have walked away from Jesus.

"Therefore, since we have so great a cloud of witnesses surrounding us, let us also lay aside every encumbrance and the sin which so easily entangles us" (Hebrews 12:1). "Looking unto Jesus, the author and finisher of our faith, who for the joy that was set before Him endured the cross, despising the shame, and has sat down at the right hand of the throne of God" (Hebrews 12:2 NKJV).

Fortunately, Jesus will never leave us or forsake us. He longs for fellowship with us every day, not just on Sundays or holidays. When Christ is our focus, He blesses us with the peace that surpasses all understanding. "You will keep in perfect peace all who trust in you, all whose thoughts are fixed on you" (Isaiah 26:3 NLT).

Father, You are so holy. Worthy are You, Lord, of all glory, honor, power, and praise. Thank you for the strength and encouragement we receive from those who bear witness to Your goodness and mercy. Forgive us for taking our eyes off You for even a moment. Keep us in perfect peace as we set our eyes on the author and finisher of our faith. In Jesus's name, amen.

Emmanuel, God with Us!

One afternoon several years ago, Oklahoma weather again delivered one of its notorious spring storms. The day had been exceptionally warm, and forecasters were warning of the potential hazard of threatening weather in late afternoon and evening. Therefore, we stayed tuned to our local weather channel.

Earlier in the day, the storm had been quite a distance southwest of our town, moving in a direction we felt would miss us entirely. As is so typical in Oklahoma, however, toward evening, the storm shifted, and suddenly we found ourselves packing up jackets, shoes, medications, and the dog, while making plans with neighbors. The storm passed directly over our heads, and in true Oklahoma form, we stood outside while looking straight up into the eye of the storm. The most eerie silence stunned its foolish audience ... and the storm was gone.

Until I remembered ... *my parents!*

My parents lived on a farm nine miles northeast of town—in the direct path of the storm. I tried to call, but no one answered. Good! That meant they were in the storm shelter. Still, I struggled between staying where I was until the storm had moved from the county or jumping in my car and racing out to my parents' place.

Then the news I feared the most came from the sheriff's office. My parent's farm had been hit by what would later be described as an F3 tornado. Arriving at their farm that evening, we were shocked by what we observed. With only the light of a full moon, we saw that every grain bin was gone, leaving only concrete slabs. The old barn was completely gone, as were many of the trees. Within twenty feet of the corner of the house was a huge sixty-year-old cedar tree with a trunk diameter of at least three feet. It looked like a wishbone split completely in half down to its base.

Since fallen power lines prevented further inspection that night, we retreated to the house to comfort one another. The rest of the night consisted of lots of coffee, quite a few tears ... but also, giving thanks to God.

You see, while the barn, the hay shed, the bins and other out buildings were completely gone, the home and one of the cars were left virtually unscathed. The car was not in the garage but rather was in the driveway right beside the now wish-boned tree. The roof sustained minor damage from flying debris, but not one window in the home was broken. It seemed nearly impossible when considering the path of the tornado and the location of the old tree that the house and car did not receive at least some damage, yet they did not. A neighbor commented later that it appeared God had laid His hand upon the house and car and said, "You cannot touch these!"

There was *no doubt* that God was with them in their storm that night.

I love the story in the Gospel of Mark where Jesus calmed the storm for his disciples. It is a wonderful example of how He can also calm the storms (or trials and ordeals) in our personal lives.

"And there arose a great storm of wind, and the waves beat into the ship, so that it was now full" (Mark 4:37 KJV).

Isn't that the way life seems to be? One minute everything is fine, and suddenly and unexpectedly, our whole world is torn apart—a phone call, a knock on the door, a lay-off notice, a grim diagnosis. The ominous waves of trepidation beat violently against us, slowly filling us with paralyzing fear and anxiety.

"And Jesus was sleeping at the back of the boat with his head on a cushion. The disciples woke him up, shouting, 'Teacher, don't you care that we're going to drown?'" (Mark 4:38 NLT).

Sometimes it appears that God doesn't really notice our storms, as if He is asleep on a cushion somewhere. Why does it seem that God takes His time when we are in an obvious state of panic?

But the disciples cried out to the Lord. "Then He arose and rebuked the wind, and said to the sea, 'Peace, be still!' And the wind ceased and there was a great calm. But He said to them, 'Why are you so fearful? How is it that you have no faith?'" (Mark 4:39–40 NKJV).

Storms reveal our true nature. They show us our utter helplessness and our total dependence upon God. They can also reveal our lack of faith. I've spoken with so many who tell of the indescribable peace of God they experienced in the midst of some very difficult storms. Fortunately, Jesus was in their boat. *They cried out* to Him and *He arose.*

It may not always be immediate; sometimes there are things we must go through in order to remove some of the junk that is hindering our walk with Christ. David said, "It is good for me that I have been afflicted; that I might learn Thy statutes" (Psalm 119:71).

Sometimes we bring on our own storms; at times other people cause them, or perhaps, like the disciples and even my parents, you simply are at the mercy of the weather, but God is always merciful and provides either protection or rescue. Remember, as the disciples learned, the presence of Jesus does not always keep our storms from coming. The Bible never promises smooth sailing; but it does promise a safe landing. Just make sure that Jesus is in your boat.

Father, life can sure deal some heavy blows, and some of us right now are going through dreadful storms. Help us remember to keep our eyes on our Savior, on the One whom even the wind and the seas obey. Thank you for hearing our cries and calming our fears in the midst of the crashing waves of sickness and disease, joblessness and depression, abandonment and injustice, etc. Teach us in our storms to place our trust in You alone. You are Emmanuel, God with us. In Jesus's name, amen.

Author's Note

God has been so gracious to me throughout my life, even when I paid no attention to Him. In 1988, in a moment of emotional and spiritual confusion, I flipped through my Bible and came across a prayer in the third chapter of Ephesians. For some reason, I was intensely drawn to read it over and over, finally even memorizing it. I had no idea why. I was not even serious about my faith in those days. After memorizing it, I did not pick my Bible up again for four years. Then, in 1992, I couldn't put it down.

Today, I know why I was so compelled to memorize the following prayer:

"For this reason I bow my knees before the Father, from whom every family in heaven and on earth derives its name, that He would grant you, according to the riches of His glory, to be strengthened with power through His Spirit in the inner man; so that Christ may dwell in your hearts through faith; *and* that you, being rooted and grounded in love, may be able to comprehend with all saints what is the breadth and length and height and depth, and to know the love of Christ which surpasses knowledge; that you may be filled up to all the fullness of God.

Now to Him who is able to do exceedingly abundantly beyond all that we ask or think, according to the power that works within us, to Him *be* glory in the church and in Christ Jesus to all generation, forever and ever. Amen."

(Ephesians 3:14–21)

This prayer accurately conveys my heart's passion and the reason behind my writings. It is my desire for you to be "rooted and grounded" in this Love. The kind of love that will lift you above your trials, calm you in the midst of storms, guide you through the maze of worldly temptations, walk with you in your valleys, and rejoice with you on your mountain tops.

The love of Christ will hold you when you are sad, lonely, or frightened; He will bind up your wounded heart and wipe away the tears. He will welcome you with open arms and a holy kiss when you reek from the stench of sin and rebellion—that kind of love. And He is the kind of love that would be spit on, be stripped of His garments, would endure thirty nine lashes with a Roman's whip and then suffer an agonizing death on the cross—just for you. That kind of Love.

I want you to know my Jesus, the power of His resurrection and the intimate fellowship of the Holy Spirit. I want you to experience the surpassing greatness of His love, filled to overflowing with all of His fullness to the glory and praise of God the Father through Jesus Christ the Son.

I hope you have enjoyed this book. I hope it stirs memories of your own childhood or parenting experiences and causes you to view your life through the lens of God's divine providence, even when you were unaware of it. I hope the next time you find a rotten potato, it will remind you of the rottenness of sin. I hope the next time you sit down to a bowl of chicken, noodles, and mashed potatoes, you will think of God's manifold blessing of mercy, peace, and love. I hope you will begin to create your own biblical parallels throughout your days.

God's creation testifies to not only His ingenious creativity, but also His unfathomable love, His indescribable beauty, magnificent grace, and boundless wonders. How great is our God. How great is His love for us. He beckons us from the moment we are conceived and follows us throughout our lives, gently drawing us to our knees. Then, in a tender moment of sweet surrender, Jesus takes our hand as we open our hearts to Him so that we might receive all that He has for us. God bless you now and forever in your marvelous journey through life's inevitable sticker patches.

Now to Him who is able to keep you from stumbling, and to make you stand in the presence of His glory blameless with great joy, to the only God our Savior, through Jesus Christ our Lord, be glory, majesty, dominion, and authority, before all time, now and forever. Amen. (Jude 24, 25)

Grace and peace always,
Shari England